Planted But Needed Water

A True Story about Faith, Resilience and Self-Belief

By Antoinette Chase

ISBN 978-1-7774662-0-6

© 2020 Antoinette Chase

All rights reserved

Dedication

This book is dedicated to my Grandmother, Aunt and all my earth angels who have played a role in my life.

Contents

Foreword 1

Preface 4

Introduction 6

Chapter One 8

   Be Thankful 8

Chapter Two 14

   How it all Began 14

Chapter Three 28

   The I Wish Moments 28

Chapter Four 34

   How many times have you tried and "failed" 34

Chapter Five 48

   The Change that Caused the Change 48

Chapter Six 59

   Hopeless yet Relentless 59

Chapter Seven 68

   The Breaking Point 68

Chapter Eight 76

   The Decision 76

Chapter Nine 85

Exercising Patience 85

Chapter Ten 102

Nothing Just Happens 102

Conclusion 115

Foreword

In this day and age, it is hard to find a young person with the ability to lead while diverting attention away from herself and unto Jesus. I met Antoinette around 2015 or 2016 at our former church. She was one of the most humorous persons I have ever met, and we just hit it off just like that! We became a family and now I am one of her Pastors. One of Antoinette's traits which I admire is that she loves people and believes everyone deserves a second chance, which is a rare trait in young adults today.

The reason I gladly endorse this book and ask that you join me in endorsing its vision is that I connected with this book from my core. Growing up in Jamaica, I experienced a lot of what Antoinette went through. Most of us at this moment may be our own worst enemy because of what we experienced as a child. I can attest that there are so many who live under similar conditions and even mentally, some are stuck in an awful cycle that is empty and sad. There are so many that have been through what Antoinette has or worse and their story did not turn out like hers. Why? She was blessed with a foundation that enabled her to stand no matter how difficult her circumstances. She is showing her generation how to get out of the rut so that they can find their pathway to peace within.

I am very thankful for this book you are about to read. It had stirred my heart again to represent God on earth as we share our testimony. We should always be prepared for spiritual warfare in whatever form it may come and most importantly the warfare within which we are equipped to handle, because when it comes to self-encounter no one knows us as we know ourselves. I believe God desires to help every one of us reach a level where we no longer fight against ourselves or be our own worst enemy. Instead, the Lord wants us to sober up and be alert so we can see His direction for every area of our lives.

In this powerful book 'Planted but needed Water" you will learn how to handle some surprising and not so surprising enemies within while building a stronger relationship with God the Father. God has been working through Antoinette's Life and he can do the same for you. Reading this book will help you to identify and become more aware of the transformation that is required for you and what will happen when you allow God to move through you so you can become the best version of yourself, which is the best that he intended for you from the beginning.

Pastor Carlene Williams

Master of Christian Life Coach (MCCL)

Order of Pastoral & Counseling (OPC)

Antoinette and I met at church and instantly became friends. We both joined the same church at the same time and since then we became closer than family as she is like a daughter to me.

Antoinette is bold and purposeful in everything she does and this is encapsulated in the way she pushed through her experiences. Her book presents everyday life situations and encourages readers who feel like they are the only ones going through these life experiences. It brought back memories of my childhood and captured my imagination as I felt like I was there, seeing and feeling everything the Author was describing.

The power of this book is that it is an encouraging tool to help all those who think they are alone and no one cares for them or about them, it will help you to change the direction of your situation for the better. Antoinette is a powerhouse of strength and sagacity and is the best person to write this book because she had harsh real-life experiences first hand and came out victoriously to talk about it to others. This is now the perfect timing, as so many people are feeling powerless in their situations but after reading this, you will move from powerless to powerful, to be able to triumph over your circumstances.

If you need solutions and want to save yourself pain and heartaches, read this book, it will give you a different outlook on life.

Bishop Basil Williams

National Deputy Bishop and Secretary for PCG Ontario

Preface

If anyone had told me that I would be an author, my first thought would be 'oh please'. I had never dreamt of writing a book that reflects my life story, but some time ago I had a vision of myself sharing my story and I felt the need to pursue this vision so I could help others. My two best friends supported this vision before I even put it on paper; I thought the idea was crazy but to them, I am crazy, not the idea. They supported me from the initial conception and now the craziness has become a reality.

I found myself in some challenging situations and now I believe I have been pulled by the unseen hand of God to encourage persons through my experiences to ignite some changes in their lives. My intention has always been to be purposeful and this book gives me purpose. I believe people's lives will be touched, there will be change and this manifestation will take place.

I remember listening to an interview with Steve Harvey and He said "A person has to remember that the road to success is always under construction" and then it hit me that from I was born, it appeared as though, I was always under construction.

I have learned that our main setbacks in life occur when we don't realize our true potential. This often appears when our back is against the wall and we have no other alternative than to fend for ourselves. We sometimes throw the biggest pity parties not acknowledging that we are under construction and someday this construction project must be over. It must now be determined when this construction project will reach completion or if there will ever be a deadline.

Introduction

This book is intended to inspire readers who have been trapped in a level of uncertainty either physically, emotionally or financially. This book is aimed at encouraging individuals to learn how to rely on themselves through internal power that one cannot explain. If you should think about it, you will understand that every bad thing that happens in your life, will either make or break you, but 98% of the time it is entirely dependent on the individual to determine the type of result they hope to accomplish.

Many of us find ourselves in motivational slumps that we have to work to get out of. Sometimes it is like a continuous cycle, where we are motivated for a period, fall out and then have to rebuild again. This gets harder each time.

This book will hopefully push you to understand that there is nothing more powerful for self-motivation than the right attitude. You cannot choose or control your circumstances all the time, but you can choose your attitude towards your circumstances. I had to develop this right mental attitude, then I found that self-motivation came naturally after this. I pray you will find this truth for yourself and be empowered to move through your all circumstances with the right attitude.

Chapter One

Be Thankful

Through the 'Power of gratitude,' I have learned how to appreciate the smallest things in life and because of this, writing this book was easy, as not having much had groomed me to be thankful.

Growing up, I never had the luxury of getting new clothes or toys, everything that I received was already worn by a few persons before me. But regardless of this, as a child, I was happy because then my feeling was that it is mine, it is new and I am the first to wear it. I was shaped by my Grandmother to be thankful and she always encouraged me to be happy and have manners in all circumstances. She instilled in us the principle of good manners and respect in all situations, so much so, that I thought this was my road out of poverty. Her repetitive 'song', which is one of her favorite quotes to use, still rings loudly in my ears today 'manners will take you through the world'. Even though she never had a high school education she had engraved some permanent instructions in my subconscious as a child, that helped me to become the woman I am today. I still have not gone 'through the world" as yet, but I trust my Grandmother, if she said it, I believed it.

I was brought up to believe that if I want something badly enough through perseverance and dedication it will happen eventually. If you should think about it, our lives do not change until we realize that it is the resilience within us that drives us. Think of a corn seed, how is it that some small seed can grow and produce so much? All you need is one corn seed in a two to three-inch soil, once this seed is planted it germinates in five to 12 days depending on the temperature. This same corn tree will have many stalks that can go up to fifteen inches and because of this one seed that was planted in whatever condition the result will be satisfying, it may take longer than the average seed to see the full production but a harvest is coming.

At some point, I could only relate to being a "hangry" (hungry and angry) plant. In Jamaica, we are known to be very descriptive and we manipulate the English language to create a visual effect of exactly how we are feeling. So being the hangry plant, that I was, I craved nourishment for survival. Just as the seed requires water and plant nutrients, so does a child. I craved the love of a Mother, the patient hand to guide me with my everyday trials, and the care and support that helps a child to grow to their full potential….I needed this and my Mama, the one who was not my Mother, provided this and more with her unconditional love. The drive to demonstrate strength through difficult times, be respectful, honest, grateful, show care and compassion was a part of the developmental skills that I had acquired from my childhood through the upbringing of my grandmother.

As children, we rely on our parents to nurture and feed us to survive in this world. Without nourishment, the leaves of a plant will suffer from nitrogen deficiency and will become withered (yellow or pale green). Like the plant, if we don't get the nourishment, we will 'dry up and dedd', as the colloquial statement in Jamaica goes, meaning, the plant will suffer and die…while this may be the extreme case for a child, the lack of nurturing does lead to great suffering.

When you think about it, some plants know how to survive in rough conditions, they merely rely on mother nature to survive. My circumstances forced me to endure through the daily hardship and I believe that irrespective of your background, the color of your skin or ethnicity once you have made a conscious decision to change your current situation the change will occur. We all have been through a place in our life where we question ourselves and asked how is that we were able to overcome.

During my research, I realized that most successful persons speak of having nothing but only a vision of themselves having everything. These success stories exist because an individual realizes that a change must happen. This to me is faith, the Bible says in James 2:14 that "Faith without works is dead." So, what are you waiting on, why do you need someone to motivate you for you to make your move? Life throws different situations at us and it is up to us to determine how to use these challenges to our advantage. Many times, the human part of us just wants to roll over and die, but there are times when that tiny part of us is there cheering us on, to fight until we have nothing left.

All my life I was given very few choices indirectly, this is to move or stay in my current situation. My home in St. Ann, Jamaica with Mama was a one-bedroom building (shack), it was framed like a house and was constructed by hand using concrete and wood. From the flooring to window height was concrete and from there upwards was wood. The roofing comprised of galvanized zinc…. this was 'naked' zinc with no maintenance, so there were holes and rust from all angles. If it rained, we had to cover our belongings with plastic bags, and when it got too hot, our cooling area was on the outside. We had no electricity or running water and because of the poorly constructed infrastructure, we had to make sure the lamp was monitored at all times. This space was shared by five persons, two adults and three children, we all could not actively be in the house at the same time unless we were sleeping because the perimeter limited our movement. This room was equipped with two beds and a table, the table was used to keep the kerosene lamp and to store food containers and utensils. Through all of this, it was a cuddly little facility, it was what I knew as home and I was happy.

This memory is stuck with me because this verified how little I had and how grateful and happy I was. I had no idea what poverty was, even though I was living it. I was nurtured to be contented, while my peers did the total opposite, I was taught never to be envious of other people's property for any reason, and if for any reason I found myself jealous of other person's things, I would have to keep it to myself and hope and pray that I don't reveal this behavior in my sleep. Being one of the three kids grown by my Grandmother she constantly reminded us that 'you never know what persons have to go through to get what they have', this warned us not to be jealous of others. In 1 Thessalonians 5:18, it says "Give thanks in all circumstances, for this is God's will for you in Christ Jesus."

Believe me, it is hard sometimes to be grateful, especially when in your head you are thinking that this was not how you had imagined your life. However, let me remind you, that they are some aspects of developing an attitude of gratitude that only come from walking through struggles. Difficulties are not meant to be roadblocks in your life—God wants to use them to transform you and make you more like Him!

It is just like a caterpillar turning into a butterfly, it is natural for us to go through a process of struggle as we experience personal transformation and are nurtured into spiritual, physical and even financial maturity. Over the years, I have learned to be thankful, especially when my life becomes full of challenges. We can develop a heart of gratitude by focusing on all the good gifts that God has given us. Being thankful has opened the doors for me on several occasions. When I wanted to migrate from Jamaica to Canada I did not know anyone in this foreign country, neither did I have financial support for the transition, but I kept trusting

God and thanking him for making the way for me and he did come through.

"Thank you" it is the key that opens the door to instant happiness, it unlocks the door to everything we are seeking in life. If we are to analyze things a bit deeper, no matter what you say you want, whether is it security, riches, health, to help others, it all boils down to the need for happiness and contentment. The truth is, we can have it now when we learn to be thankful. There was a time in my life when all I could do was hope that my circumstance will change. I was experiencing high levels of stress from my first marriage that led me to isolated depression. I was abused financially and physically but kept it to myself because I was embarrassed for anyone to find out. This was even more difficult because of the image I believed that I had to maintain for the church and persons looking in.

Regardless of this, I stood my ground and I continued to be grateful, then a good friend of mine introduced me to "The Secret' this was an audiobook that changed my life. I had the attitude to be thankful and content but there was something that was still missing and even though I considered myself as a Christian woman of faith, I found myself doubting God's promises. I would weep daily and in the back of my head, I was still thankful because I believed that my situation will groom me to become stronger.

Chapter Two

How it all Began

We are often encouraged to push past our pain. When giving birth, it was so annoying to hear the Doctor and nurses say 'push, push you are almost there', when deep down you just want that child out of you. You want to kick scream and yell but unless you take pain medicine you will just have to push through that pain. It is just like any situation you may find yourself in, it will all begin with pain or some level of discomfort but after that pain, you will see that joy and understand that you needed to endure the agony to experience the reward.

I was born in the heart of Kingston, Jamaica to a single mother who had me at age seventeen (17), I never knew my father or anyone that was related to him. My mother then left me with her stepmother when I was three (3) months old. She raised me and I called her Mama because she was the only mother I knew. She heard my first word, saw the first step, and she even breastfed me as this was her way of comforting me at that age. I can't imagine how rough it must have been on her. When my child was three (3) months old, her neck strength was just improving when she is held upright, she ate more and she also demanded more attention. A baby is a 24 hours full-time job and I can only imagine what Mama had to deal with, but she was able to find ways to take care of me in a one-bedroom shack that was shared with four (4) other persons.

Although Mama was a widow and self-employed, she made every effort to ensure that her family was taken care of. Her livelihood came from selling ground provisions at the market. She was relentless, strong-willed and determined; I am yet to see anyone as strong as her, she would carry her produce back and forth on her head or shoulder for miles, she never complained about being tired or in pain even on her death bed. The process of preparing for the market every week was a task by itself. We would travel by foot to various farms for the ground provision and transport these yams, potatoes and bananas on our heads back to the village……. our feet, hands and heads were our biggest asset. (While using a donkey, like other higglers would have been more feasible, we could not afford one.) The produce was then packed in "crocus bags" stacked with a cross for protection and labelled. We then waited for hours on the streetside for the Market Truck to take us to Browns Town Market.

I often wonder how is it that she was able to keep us in line, as well as other children that she had grown in the community, There was no male figure around to help her, but she knew what was supposed to be done and she went out and did it. She made sure that her home was kept in order and although the obvious struggle was there, we were trained to be content.

You may have been in tough situations before and wondered how you got out. The simple explanation is that you had it in you from your early childhood, you may have just repressed that ability. Don't give up on life when things get tough, sometimes we have to push ourselves to see our limits.

Back in the 80s in my area, tap or running water was a luxury, privacy did not exist and the ability to choose what to eat was taboo, you ate what was available without complaints. My one-bedroom shack was located in what was referred to as 'deep bush' in the heart of rural Jamaica. Our means of transportation were our legs or donkeys, we had no street lights so we relied on bottle torches or kerosene lamps to guide us through our dark and dusty streets. The dirt tracks that we used as roads were paved with stones and red clay, which posed challenges for a motor vehicle(s) to operate in the area. For drinking water, we had to gather water from the pond which was approximately (8) miles from our dwelling.

In a house with a mixture of adults and children, we had to be creative with entertainment along with our daily lifestyle. We would play in the streets at night under sheets, pretending to be ghosts. This was often after listening to all sorts of ghosts (duppy) stories. If we wanted to watch television, the only option was to walk twenty (20) minutes to half an hour to see one at a corner shop in the community.

Our bathroom was behind trees or bushes, it varied based on the time of day. We would bathe on the outside at nights so that no passer-by can see us clearly and, in the morning, we bathed before sunrise for school. This process entailed finding some high bushes or trees to hide behind so we could get some level of privacy. We then used a bucket or bottle of water and very efficiently washed ourselves. Food preparation was done on the outside beneath a few pairs of zincs, just enough to cover the wooded fire from rain and dust.

Our dining area was outside which I must admit was fun when we were having meat for dinner. With all of this, I do not remember ever complaining about not being satisfied or even hungry. When we are about to eat, it was the custom to bless our food first even when we are eating only bread and sugar and water for dinner. Mama was a strong woman of faith and she was relentless, even though I never saw her attending church, I could never be absent. I once asked her why we needed to pray all the time? she said to us that 'many children did not have bread and we are living like queens so we have to pray and thank God for his goodness'. This principle of always being thankful remains in my life to this day, I am always giving thanks regardless of how small my blessing may seem. I often say a blessing is a blessing big or small, it is spelled the same way. I have learned to be thankful and content regardless of what was happening around me. I am just as excited about what some may deem as small, as I am about the big ones because I have learned to appreciate the little that I have and I have mastered the art of living without.

I believe that it takes some hidden superpower to take care of your children, and even more so with other people's children, but Mama managed to do that and more. Even though she was not very educated, she was strict about us going to school to get an education. Sometimes we were not equipped for school, we had no shoes, books, or even money to buy food but she implemented one of the best strategies for school supplies. Mama would cut an exercise book and a pencil in half so that each person had a book for school or at least, half of a book for school. We had to go barefooted and if we did not have lunch money we would go to school and then return home for lunch then head back to school for the next period.

She was excellent in managing her time as well as ours; we had to do chores, study and stay humble in whatever situation we found ourselves in. One might ask how can an uneducated woman develop so many strategies to ensure that her home is run right? How is it that we never ended up on the wrong side of the law? How is it that we were able to grow even with little or no finances? But God has a way of choreographing our circumstances on an individual basis, we may not know how it is going to happen but all we have to do is trust the process.

You need not worry when things are not working out the way how you want it to, God can work through impossible situations.

I have lived to see him showing up for me in more ways than one. My life then, could have forced me to become toxic and rebellious as there were many opportunities for this to happen but

I had a vision of myself that I needed to see manifested. I often see circumstances change to my advantage and I know that it has to be a higher creator. Imagine, with no access to clean water, security and medical we managed to survive the hardship of growing up. We hear of persons complaining now about child labor but back in the '80s these words were never around. If you can walk and if you have hands and a head that means you are blessed to carry something. With a rigid day to day activity from one farm field to the next, and from pond to spring, these were the fittest days of my life. Keep in mind that we were doing all this while travelling barefooted. Thankful for the mechanism that God created in our bodies where the more we walked on the hot stones and thorns the thicker the bottom of our feet became. After a while our feet adapted to the environment, we could see scales and scabs on the outer layer of our feet but this was normal in my community.

Just like how our bodies adapt to a specific environment, we have to learn how to be adaptable, you may believe that you are delicate but I believe that God has created you to trample through any situation. Brace for impact, as rough times can feel incredibly overwhelming and exhausting; but there are many things you can do to soften the blow if you are currently not in crisis but have issues to work through, I would recommend you seek help. In my case I choose to get involved in various community activities, I surrounded myself with people who had similar interests plus I had a great relationship with my church community.

"It's best to fix the roof when the sun is shining", according to JF Kennedy, I believe this applies to when we are dealing with our childhood issues, relational issues, or anything else. When we are in periods of relative calm, it may be the best investment of time and effort we can make, and when ready, we must look for the lessons learned. It is often said that difficulties or hardships are stepping stones for advancement which in return gives us a learning experience, believe it or not, these variables deepen our understandings of ourselves, others, and the world around us. We may not believe it but they are hidden blessings that come with every hardship, such as strength, wisdom, empathy or openness to a deeper awareness.

Sometimes we borrowed our neighbor's pungent 'pit' latrine to relieve ourselves and this was only when permission was received to proceed. Just so you have an idea of what a pit latrine is, it's also known as "pit toilet" or "long drop", is a type of toilet that collects human faeces in a hole in the ground. Urine and faeces enter the pit through a drop hole in the floor, which might be connected to a toilet seat or squatting pan for user comfort, this was also built to function without water. If they said no, we would head back to the bushes and find a comfortable stone to do our business.

This was the norm to me; I grew up seeing everyone doing this, so I was in my comfort zone. I believed that this was how other families did it, but little did I know that we were exposed to all sorts of diseases. The great thing about all of this is that I believed that we have developed some strong immune system to fight any virus because we were never sick, my grandma lived up until she was Eighty-nine (89) years old. The things we now take for granted are the things that I never had, and in some parts of the world, we still have children who are living in the conditions that I used to live in, over Thirty (30) years ago.

So, what are you doing about that? What can we do about it? Are we going to sit back and pretend as if these issues aren't real? How can you help? We all have a part to play and we need to reflect and do some self-analysis.

The use of clean water, the right to privacy and not to mention the right to choose what to eat,… reading this now you are probably saying how was I able to get out of an environment that restricted me to such conditions? When I think about it, the environment physically was not suitable to live in for any human, but mentally I was in a place of contentment, I was surrounded by love and support from my guardian, through all the hiccups I was given compassion and respect. She took care of me the best way she knew.

You may find yourself in a situation that you cannot understand how you got there or why is it that you are going through this process, but hang in there, life has a way of teaching you lessons that you are not prepared for. Just learn everything you can and do not be swallowed by your current situation. Through it all, like me, you will be able to say those were some of the best days of your life......well, maybe not best, but it did teach you some valuable lessons.

I have mastered the art to live in any situation and to cope with any individual, I am not easily impressed by material things, I know what it is like to have nothing, I know what it is like to be homeless and neglected and most of all I know how it is to survive with little or no support. I was born in it and I grew up in it, but I chose not to stay in it. Your social development should not hinder you from your goal. Do not be a victim of your family's legacy, if your parents were underprivileged or violent, do not allow that to dictate your life or how you raise your own family. Do not allow anyone to tell you that you can't make it or you will end up just like your 'worthless mother or father' (this was a very popular statement that parents told their children repeatedly).

Every challenge we face is all in our head and each obstacle gets tougher when it has manifested in the physical realm, this is where it is more than a mental challenge. For instance, we may have issues with something as simple as falling asleep, where medication is required for sleep or the ability to move freely but not able to because we developed various acute illnesses relating to stress. There was a time I had constant headaches for days that prevented me from sleeping, I was scared of everything and anyone that breathes and I lived in fear for an extended period in my life, so I know the mental battles we all go through and I also know that when these are not dealt with, we become prone to the physical challenges that come on us. If we believe it is not there, it will not be there, if we tell people life is hard, then it will only get harder. Speak positive things in your life, in your children's lives and watch how God will open doors for you. The word of God said life and death are in the power of the tongue and whatever it is that you bind on earth is bound in heaven. Can you imagine having a power that allows you to speak to your situation and watch changes manifest in front of your eyes?

Mama knew what she was instilling in us, she was a vendor, popularly known as "Higgler" in the Jamaican culture. We would go to the market with her sometimes and this was one of my favorite things to do because I would get my share of the load to sell ground produce, and the profit from these sales would be mine. Mama was grooming me for success at this tender age, this was my own money…. just imagine as an eight-year-old how rich that made me feel because I was able to have my own cash that I could use to buy lots of ice cream and colorful sweets. I was the talk of the market whenever I would go with Mama. My aunt often tells the story of how mad she got at me because all my stuff would be sold off before hers and she couldn't understand why. The truth is that my customers never really wanted what I was selling but because I was so tiny and was deemed very bold, tenacious and polite (they would say I was prime), they would often purchase from me. This was a lesson to me, that no matter how things seem dim, doors have a way of opening up even when it is bolted, chained and sealed. My aunt still tells stories of how mama would be on her face the entire day with no sales and as I sat with her persons from all angles would just show up.

You may not know what your destiny is, you may not even understand why it is that you have to struggle harder than everyone else, but I encourage you to press on, your timing will come and when it comes you may not even be qualified for it, but it will be for you and no one can take away your moment.

Even though my Grandmother never had much education, nor was she a regular churchgoer, she gave lots of love and guidance, she ensured that we were in Sunday school, and we couldn't even be absent from school either. She insisted on us getting an education and the transaction would not be completed unless God is in the midst of it all. After years of going barefooted, I was eventually given a pair of shoes. Unlike other Children who had shoes and clothes for special occasions, I was blessed with this one all-purpose shoe, rain or shine, that was the only shoe I had. The shoe was made from leather by the community shoemaker, so it was sturdy. Sometimes because of the climate, my feet got so hot and uncomfortable I had to take it off and carry it in my hands. This was no issue to me because I had grown accustomed to being barefooted.

Many times, we get so complacent in our situation that when we are out of it we do not know how to behave. Life as we know it is made up of different stages and we are sometimes forced to accept it or just sit and watch the stages grow past us. The good thing about all the rough stages that come with this journey called life is that it prepares you mentally, physically, spiritually, and emotionally to deal with the future.

Think about it, like a marathon that you are training for, you want to win but you have no idea if you will win because you may not be aware of who will be in the race or how well trained they are and even what to expect at the actual competition. There are lots of uncertain factors that lie ahead, no matter how fit you are or how well trained you are you never know when you may pull a hamstring (pull a muscle). We may say we need a track record but how is that we're going to get a record if we are not willing to face the track? Make a move, expect the unexpected and deal with it when it comes.

It hasn't been easy, I mean through these periods, I have mastered the art of how to take care of my belongings or suffer the consequences, be contented, be grateful and most of all to be respectful and honest. After several years' experience of going to school barefooted and going back home for lunch then back to school, it became a part of me. This was the norm that was my lifestyle and hence the contentment. How many times have we been in a situation which seems like forever that becomes a part of our lifestyle, and we had to make a conscious decision on whether to stay in what we are accustomed to or make a decision to get out of that position?

You may wonder why was it is that we had to leave school and return home for lunch, this was not a choice but it was merely because we had no other options, lunch allowance was a luxury, we could not pack food and take to school because we did not have the facilities for that. We were fortunate in the '80s and '90s because we had nutriments that were given to us in school from the government in those days. There were trucks with bun (called bullas) and milk that went to the public schools daily with crates of these nutriments to distribute to children. I used to take as much as I could get and take back home because dinner was not always guaranteed.

With all of this, I can still hear my Mama reiterating in our heads, stories of how God close the mouth of lions for Daniel, part the red sea for Moses, make the sun stood still for Joshua, open the Prison for Peter, put a baby in the arms of Sarah and raise Lazarus from the dead. She was not an active Christian but she believed that all things were possible if we only believe. Then she would have closed her stories by saying it is not impossible for God to do wonders in our lives, her words have kept me secure throughout my childhood days and even as an adult I can remind myself that my problems are small for my mighty God.

I have learned to understand that even though we may display similar characteristics, we were all created amazingly special and unique, so why be discouraged or try to change the person that you are, why live in distress when God has lined up prosperity for you? Have you ever been in a place where you knew that something is in store for you but you are uncertain of what and when it will come through? That's me, I get so impatient at times because I think my change is taking too long, my thing is that I want things to happen on my timing and I had to learn that I don't always have control over every aspect of my life.

If we are to be honest with ourselves, we sometimes are so impatient that we want to walk in other people's shoes even if we don't understand their situation or how they got their shoes. I often hear my grandmother say that 'small minds can't comprehend big spirits and to be great one has to be willing to be mocked, hated and even misunderstood', back then this made no sense to me. Your greatness is just around the corner but your time is never God's time. Allow yourself to go through the various segments in your life it is normal to question it and ask why us, but we have to go through these times to help someone else or even make ourselves stronger.

When our neighbours were making additions to their houses and eating rice and peas, we were contented with our yam and scallion or our dumplings and butter. Again, Mama would ensure that we bless our food and would encourage us not to be jealous of the sweet aroma that we were inhaling from our neighbor's kitchen. It's natural to ask questions as kids and even be jealous, nevertheless, we maintained a level of gratitude not by choice but because we were trained that way.

Chapter Three

The I Wish Moments

I have had several moments that I would say "oh my gosh I wish that was me," but I have learned and strongly came to the realization that they are times when God will put someone in front of us who has exactly what we want, just to see how we will respond.

Until we can pass His "I am happy for you" test, we are never going to have any more than what we have right now. Most times if he blesses us with what we think we desire or will make us happy we will lose our purpose. Sometimes our purpose in life is to go through life with nothing so we may be able to inspire each other. Sometimes we just need to spend less time comparing our book to someone else's and spend more time developing and advancing our own story

I am not saying that it is not ok to be jealous and to want to have some luxury, absolutely nothing is wrong with that as long as your jealousy has boundaries, meaning, you will not hurt persons or go out of your way to get what you think you deserve. The spirit of envy and maliciousness does not respect anyone and once you allow it to take residence in your space, this can grow within you then transfer into your children and grandchildren's lives.

People often ask me if I would change anything about my childhood days, and the answer to that is always no. I'm a strong believer of the fact that your current situation will never determine your outcome in life. People often talk about generational curse but some scholars even think the generational curse is a myth.

I believe that not because my parents are poor, I would end up poor and because my mother had me at seventeen that doesn't mean that this will happen to me. I can vividly remember in my teenage years when I was about fourteen (14) years old, I was told that I will never become anything in life by my birth Mother. I was told that I am not learning anything in school and I was just wasting her money; I remember having to go to school without the basic necessity because to my mother it was pointless. But if I should be biblical, my favorite book spoke about the children of the Israelites when they were trapped in the wilderness and what they did, they shouted and believed that they would get their breakthrough. I knew my wilderness would not last forever, on a hungry stomach I would still show up for school, I went to school without writing books but someone always showed up for me, even when I was on the edge of falling.

As humans, we tend to be skimpy with our praise, with our level of gratitude and how we choose to show our appreciation. At times when we become so ungrateful, we fail to accept how we were created and the situations we were born in. The bible mentioned that we were created in his image yet we complain about how we look, our size, and our skin color even our gender. "I wish I had the opportunity like" is a famous saying we often use. What if we tried to change the way we think, this is by taking the time to say thank you for my well-toned buttocks or my thin waste, my full figure and the little I have that I know when I get the massive I will know how to use it wisely.

It is hard to say, 'I am not jealous of anyone else or envious of what others have'. I can proudly say that God gave it to them, and I want them to enjoy it. According to the book of Hebrews, "Let your conduct be without covetousness; be content with such things as you have" I believe God tests us to see if we will live by this verse.

I have personally looked at my life and say why is it that I am working so hard? I tried to live a life with integrity, honesty and yet still instead of going forward it seems as if I am moving backwards. It is like I'm been short-changed! There are times the more effort I put out the further back I found myself. But what I always find amazing is that when I compare myself to someone else, I am in a better situation even if it's just an edge. Sometimes it's hard to compare your situation with others because you get so disappointed with your current output. But sometimes if you just take the time to listen to another person's story and hear their struggles you will see how tiny your issue is.

There have been times when I had to catch myself and recognize who is in control and the reason I am breathing. I remember praying so hard, even fasting at times for things I believed I needed from God. Many times I would murmur and ask why He hasn't given it to me yet, is it because He is 'holding out' on me? have you ever been at this place? If you have been in this place rest assured, he is not. He simply wants to make sure that you rid yourself of jealousy and make Him your top priority. Believe it or not, God's intention is for us to prosper and achieve in every way. He wants people to see His goodness and how well He takes care of us, at least that is how I understand it. It took me years to figure this out, with lots of down moments that came out with satisfactory results.

It is hard, but we must desire God more than we desire His blessings according to the book of Hebrews, we often only seek him when we find ourselves in difficulties but if we promise to be content and exercise patience we will be surprised how God will redirect our destiny.

The house structure we lived in could be classified as 'shabby' and I would always wish I had so much money that I could buy my grandmother a house. I couldn't wait to grow up and start earning so much that I could take care of her the way she took care of us. She sacrificed so much for me so that I could be a young lady. I never got the chance to tell her thanks, I never got the chance to build that castle for her, she never got the chance to see me turn sixteen, oh "I wish I could".

My grandmother was my best friend, she taught me to be strong, honest and independent. I had no female or male role model up to age fourteen (14), she was the only hero I knew and I aspired to be like her. I wanted her to feel accomplished, to be proud of me, so I thought being successful at the common entrance examinations would be my reward to her. On receiving the results that I was successful at the exams, with excitement and delight I rushed to give Mama the great news. At that time Mama had gone to the hospital to do a few checks so I rushed to the hospital to tell her I was successful, but she was not in her bed. I remember searching the entire floor for her because I thought they had released her without telling us, her bed had obvious new sheets on it and her belongings were not on the side table where we left them the previous day. With tears flowing down my aunt's cheeks, she looked at me with disbelief and concern, but I did not stick around to enquire why she was crying I kept searching for Mama with my results in my hands and joy on my face, not knowing that a simple check-up at the hospital had turned into a check out for a lifetime. Oh 'I wish I could' change a few things, if you have lost someone then you will know exactly how it is to have those moments that you could make a wish and suddenly things just snap back into place.

I just want to encourage you that pain and failures are both a normal part of life, like everything else it will pass. Worrying and overthinking will not change anything. Your tears and scars will show your strength, not your weakness, I believe that every little struggle matters, nothing is wasted, don't let other people's negative energy get to you, remember that's not your problem let them deal with their negative energy and you focus on building yourself until you are strong enough to build someone else.

For a tree to be able to stand strong enough to deal with any condition it needs a seed, it also needs soil, it must be planted and some level of nurturing must take place. Roots provide structural anchorage to keep trees from toppling over, it supplements other parts of the tree which in return is healthy for the environment. My childhood groomed me into being an adult before I was at the required age, I was an entrepreneur at the age of eight (8) years old, I knew if I sold enough ground produce, I will have enough money to buy ice cream and candies. I knew that to get this sweet fetish satisfied I would have to work tirelessly. I overcame, I developed the skill of talking my way out of trouble most times and this is because of the early nutrients that were provided to me by mama.

Chapter Four

How many times have you tried and "failed"

How you view failure is entirely dependent on you, we often believe that we fail when we did not succeed the first time when we make an attempt at something or when we did not meet our family's expectations. You will always have someone that you will never be able to please no matter how often you try. I was at a point in my life where I desperately sought approval from others, I needed to be liked so at least in my head it would be easier for my mother to like me. Herbert Bayard Swope said 'I can't give you a sure-fire formula for success, but I can give you a formula for failure, try to please everybody all the time."

I was cursed for my very existence by the person who brought me into this world, just to say that it is the smallest of all seeds that sometimes becomes the largest of garden plants; which eventually grows into a tree that birds come and make nests in its branches. I used this to say even though I had no biological father around me and a mother that resented my mere existence, I lived to see her thank God for me every day. The child that she wanted to dump and abused physically, repeatedly turned out to be her shelter and her caregiver without expecting anything in return.

My experience has taught me that, curses and abuses are sometimes what drives us into our true potentials if we only just face the man in the mirror, and acknowledge that you were made in God's image and you are what you think about and you can do anything you want especially if you have the will power. What has kept me going were my lessons as a child, despite having no shoes and little or no finances, education was a must and so was making it out of 'poverty'. Please be reminded that my educational lesson was not only from a classroom, but this was also mixed with street knowledge, Sunday school and even in the very marketplace every Friday night and Saturday morning. We often believe that we have to be in a classroom with professors and instructors to gain the knowledge we require for the world but I disagree. Some of my biggest lessons came from the higglers on the market truck going to Browns Town Market. Some of these lessons were not taught to me in University or any other classroom setting.

Those experience has molded me into what I call a strong individual, someone who can fight against all odds, someone who never gives up when everyone expects her to give up but it was not always like this. I have attempted to kill myself on several occasions, for various reasons. I remember one night… I must have reached my boiling point and this was the first attempt on my life. My neighbours and I went to a church convention this was about fifteen (15) minutes from where we were living on Maxfield Avenue, the convention ended around 9:30 PM, I got home about 10 pm, this was with adult supervision as I was about fourteen (14) years old.

When I got home, I realized that the main gate to the tenement yard that we lived in was locked, normally the gates aren't closed until midnight because that was the system that the landlord had in place. The gate was locked, so in my dress coming from church, I had to jump the 14 feet fence which was covered with broken bottles, these bottles were placed on the fence to prevent criminals or trespassers from coming over. I had no choice, if I stayed out, I was guaranteed a whipping and if I'm late from coming in I will still get a whipping. With my knees bruised and hands filled with splinters and laceration, I went in the house bleeding only to see my mom with the machete. Her only concern was that I made 10 pm catch me on the road, she gave me a few slaps across my back with the tool; ...I am still feeling them up to this point. The same night after I settled in with my slap and cuts from my very adventurous night, I heard her arguing with her boyfriend, I could hear pans throwing and furniture moving, not sure what the argument was about but she then returned to the little area that we were sleeping and all I felt was someone choking the life out of me. At this point, I was already in pain so I decided to grab a knife which was close to where our bunk bed was and I shoved it directly in my navel. I'm not sure how I'm still alive but God had a plan for me, at that point I had gotten enough and could bear no more of the physical abuse.

I could not live up to her expectations, she constantly told me how skinny I was, she wished she had flushed me when I was born.... there was nothing positive from her, so I was unhappy. It took me a while to understand that I am unique and I can't live in other people's dreams. Being the first child for my Mother I was expected to carry more than I could handle. I never knew my biological father, so up to this age I was only seeing men going back and forth from my dwelling but none at the time was a father figure, because they never lasted long.

For years, even now I still mourn the passing of my mentor, my best friend my Mama, she has left me on a solid foundation of bricks so that I can face any storm. These bricks may lose its color and texture but it continues to stay in place. Don't ever allow anyone to tell you that you are weak, you are as strong as you make yourself. My challenges would weaken me, but then somehow, I got the courage to drag myself out of it. Believe in yourself and stand up for yourself, be your own crowd cheering you on. After all, no one can cheer for you louder than you, get your pom-poms, hold them up and make noise, let them think you are losing it.

Stop relying on a spouse, family or even friends to validate your strength, you determine how strong you are, only you will be able to tell your tolerance level. As women, irrespective of race, ethnicity or religion our problems are related, we have the same if not similar stories regarding early adulthood. The process we had to go through when we are no longer a girl but a woman; just remember the process may be different but the experiences are the same. So gone are the days when we hide behind men to fight for us, when you have problems you deal with them, you don't play victim, you don't make yourself look pitiful, you don't point fingers. We stand and deal, you face the world with a head held high and carry God in your heart.

When I got my first pair of shoes, this was specifically designed for me it was made to handle any condition, it was made a few inches big so my feet could grow in it. I tried several times to wreck it because I hated it so much. But that shoe would not budge, the only way I could get rid of that shoe is for my feet to grow faster and that in itself was a challenge. I am 38 years old and my shoe size is still six (6). The point I am trying to make is when you are strong holistically not even an army consisting of David's mighty men will be able to conquer you. Now with this shoe, I was the happiest child in the district because the thought of having my feet covered for school and church occasionally was amazing. I started thinking that at least getting splinters and cracked foot bottom would now be a thing of the past. Have you ever seen yourself in a position, in your head you believe that you have accomplished what you want and you are in your safe place and then… boom, you wake up and realize that it was just your imagination?

Simply put, there was a point in my life where I believed that it was the norm to not have necessities such as clean water, a toilet and the right to privacy. Even though living in Kingston was an upgrade from where I was coming from, I still had to push carts to fetch water from other communities because no water was coming from the pipes that were in the tenement yard. A tenement yard is a big yard space that is comprised of 5 or more families living and sharing facilities.

I was upgraded from using stones, pit latrine, or bushes to a partial toilet, this was partly because it had the toilet seat but you needed to fetch water to flush and this was used by several other families. I looked at this as an upgrade because I never had to ask permission to use the facilities.

We often find ourselves in situations that we believe are impossible to get out of, we pray for change, and when the change comes it comes with lots of headaches and pain. I knew that life was changing right in front of my eyes. I was no longer a kid and maturing into a lady and the person who I have known my entire life had gone. I was forced to operate in a different environment under different management. Generally, people do not like changes even when it is for the best, we tend to have mixed reactions. As a child, I was no different. I was mad at God for taking away the one person I loved, and now I was living with a woman that I hardly knew, who gave me up when I was three (3) months old.

I eventually convinced myself that this was a good thing, I was living in the city now not the countryside and I would be able to have a better life. It is ok to be wishful; chances are you will come to terms with yourself and realize that you are only fooling yourself. People change and so should your frame of mind. There has to come a time when you have to quit fantasizing and put yourself in the position to be blessed.

I used to fantasize about living in Kingston, wondering what it would be like to live in the city, to have meat for dinner every night around a table, having clean water with my family and taking a shower but that is all it was, a fantasy. Then I was of the impression that Kingston was a rich place and the opportunities were endless there, I thought persons never had a challenge and the grass was greener there, talk about perception.

I thought because my mother was from Kingston, I shouldn't be in wants because all the opportunity in the world was there, she told my Mama that she had to live in Kingston to give me a better opportunity. Little did I know that the grass is not always greener on the other side. I would spend summer holidays with her, she had other children, so then we thought it would be good to get to know them and her which in fact should have been a great experience for me but it was not.

I sometimes believed that my mother tried to take care of me but it was so hard to understand her methods. She would gather lots of second-hand clothes for me to carry back to the country which I was happy for, but I couldn't understand how it is that I would get the old clothes, shoes and clips and my other siblings would get new ones. I was happy nevertheless because I was getting things I never had.

When I was twelve (12) years old my mother's friends finally encouraged her to take me to live with her full time because in their eyes I was turning into a young lady and my Grandmother was getting older and was less capable of taking care of me. Unhappy with the idea, I eventually moved to Kingston to live with her, then a year after my Aunt, who is my mom's smaller sister came and grandma came as well. Mama was getting older and she was not as strong as she used to be so they thought it was a good idea to have her in Kingston so that she will be better-taken care of.

Life as we knew it got even harder, it was ok for us to be living in one room on top of each other in the country where we were happy but for a better lifestyle, we moved. The tottered dilapidated one room that we called home was opening in halves after we experienced Hurricane Gilbert in 1988. So, the living situation became more hazardous.

They were huge cracks in the walls and when it rained, we would have to set containers in the house, sometimes it was so bad that we would sleep with plastic covers just in case it rained when we were sleeping. The challenges that you face now are temporary so brace yourself for greater challenges ahead. Sometimes we find ourselves in some situations that we believe can't get any worst, but I guarantee you that the older you get the more experiences you will have, and these experiences will not come with guidelines or instructions. You have to be creative and find possible solutions.

I believed that we set our destiny and if you want to make life better for yourself you can do it. Successful people do what they need to do when they feel like giving up, you must not confuse your path with your destination, just because it is stormy, it does not mean that you are not heading to sunshine.

Growing up in rural Jamaica, we were so poor that we had to take turns wearing even underwear, we had one size that would fit all; my aunt Janice was the oldest so her panty would be used by myself and my other cousin because I was tiny mama had to put bumps or a knot at each side to keep it on my waist. When the bumps would loosen, I would just pull it in place or even sometimes took it off and carried it in my hand. I may not have numerous underwear now but thanks be to God I do not have to share anymore, and if I have to take it off, it is by choice. The bottom line is that what we want in life is entirely dependent on us and how we intend on getting there.

Because you were born in a situation, it does not mean that you have to inherit the negativity that comes with the territory. I knew that God had a plan for my life I'm still not sure what that plan is; but I'm certain that everything that I had been through was a learning process to make me a better person, to encourage others and to share my testimonies with persons who have been in a worst or similar situation.

My Grandmother always boasted about me saying that I will be the one to take care of her when she gets older and I grew up with that responsibility; I felt that I had a higher purpose, and I refused to be a victim of any circumstance. She (Mama) was preparing me for a world I knew nothing about, she would give me allowance for school, when she could, which was just enough to buy "nutri-buns" and milk. Out of that little that she gave me I would go back home with change. Now, sometimes I find myself hardly making ends meet, but I able to stretch my paychecks in ways that I can't even explain. Those lessons have molded me and that is why as parents we have to be careful of what we speak into our children and what we teach them.

I admire persons and their accomplishments; however, I strongly believe that some persons have to fight or push harder to get what they want. As humans we were created to be happy and to feel good about ourselves… we must feel good about ourselves, or eventually, we will develop some sort of unhealthy, uncontrolled behavior to get the good feelings we crave.

Unfortunately, most of us still live with the burden of shame, even though the word of God assures us that we can be free of it (Isaiah 61:7). A person who is addicted to drugs probably began using them because their pain was so intense, they felt compelled to get rid of it, even if only temporarily. The same thing is true about drinking or using food as a comfort. If we do not get good feelings from the inside, then we attempt to create them through outside means. This sometimes includes choosing the wrong company or even lowering our standards just to fit in.

When your heart desires something, no matter how old you get or how far life takes you, you will find yourself working towards getting that desire that you had. What we may forget is, if we have strong needs, we will do whatever it takes to ensure those needs are met. I believe that if someone needs a blessing, they truly have to decide to move out of their comfort zone and push towards what they truly desire. We are sometimes so set on wanting the finished product, but we are lazy to go through the process of getting the finished goods.

We were raised to be contented in every situation and as a result of how I was raised by my Grandmother, the decision to be a better person was natural. I knew I had a story, hence the decision to share my life. I often asked God why was it that my mother hated me or was it that she did not know how to nurture me? Why was it that I never met my father? Those are questions that I'm yet to get answered, however, what I do know is that throughout my life, the Almighty always sends someone to take care of me. For example, the old lady that raised me was not my biological grandmother, she was my mother's stepmother. I knew my biological grandmother but I was kept away from her for reasons I still don't know. Every family has drama and mine was filled with it.

At times we feel so discouraged and alone but if we exercise our faith, we will understand we are never alone and most of all there is someone somewhere who has it worse than you and they are surviving. So why can't you? Go through your situation and teach your children how to be independent and self-conscious as early as possible. As an adult, I tend to reflect more on my childhood days; through these experiences, I can navigate my way through many difficult moments, hence the reason I believe that it is imperative for us as parents to create great standards for our children.

Mastering the art of economizing, in my opinion, is an acquired skill and to be excellent at it you must have some level of experience. In my case, my financial and social background influenced my behavior and the direction of my path. Please be aware of the fact that not all children will use their personal development as a medium to uplift themselves but I chose to do that. If I could live my life again, I would not change it for anything, because it has made me stronger.

After moving to Kingston, things began to change in various ways. I thought I would now get some information about my father or even get the chance to meet him but I did not know that my father was dead. My grandmother did not know either, and after several discussions with my mom, she eventually told me he died. I never met him, I knew no one from his side of the family, until this day my mother will not speak about him or where he was from.

I grew up knowing several step-fathers; some for months, some for years but that did not shape my future. My life in Kingston was supposed to be "greener pastures'; looking at the position that I found myself in, it was a better lifestyle I believed, I had access to 'better' care, such as clean water, a bit more privacy but with all those perks came major challenges.

We were abused physically and verbally daily, I was ready to run away back to the countryside, in fact, I even ran away from home a few times because of the abuse from my mom. Was this what greener pastures looked like? No child or elderly person should ever experience such bitterness and hostility. I believe that one of the reasons my Mama ended up in the hospital was because of the living condition and the abuse that came from my mom. She was not happy, she often said she wanted to die but in her old house, at least she knew she would be happy but I was so young to understand where this was coming from.

This abusive environment was very new for all of us, growing up in the country I was never abused by my Grandmother neither by my aunt, even when we could not find food to eat, frustration was never manifested by abuse. Mama was never angry at us; she would never tell us to go and hunt it. If you agree, one would say the true test of faith started at this stage, how do we deal with a new environment, new rules, new people, new social backgrounds, new opportunities… hopefully and most of all new influences? Do you think that who you are today has to do with how you were brought up as a child?

In the book of (Jeremiah 1: 5), it says, "Before I formed you in the womb, I knew you, and before you were born, I consecrated you; I have appointed you a prophet to the nations." I'm a strong believer that nothing happens by chance, and at times we are forced to walk in our destiny because the position or the place where we believe we are, is not what God has intended for us. We desire a new look, but are we willing to accept the various factors that may come with the new 'look' or even the new environment?

Chapter Five

The Change that Caused the Change

My life changed when I moved to Kingston...my heart desired a move to the city because in my head it was better than my previous life. Little did I know that in life, the higher you got the more risks and issues you may encounter. Having to deal with a mother that did not want me around, and this was verbalized several times as her favorite thing to say was that "she regrets not dumping or flushing me", in addition to the various abuse and violence that was evident from all corners was more than the change I expected. Kingston 13 at that time was known for the homes of criminals and gangs, but I survived it. I have lost a few relatives and friends to gang violence but God had a calling on my life.

We were surrounded by constant gunfights between streets, I was trapped in the center because the school that I attended then was at the border of the two gangs that were always in conflicts. Based on the location of our space in the tenement yard, other families in the yard who were involved in the gang would hide guns under my bed and as the day began to dawn you would see police and gunmen exchanging bullets, not caring if they would hurt innocent persons. Most nights the safest place to sleep was the floor because anything could happen when it got dark.

Separate from the outside factors, home was not comfortable for me, being a teenager, I was forced to do the duties of an adult. I would be cooking, doing laundry and taking care of my sister at the age of thirteen (13), while mom was at work. I was the 'head cook and bottle washer' as the saying goes, with the bonus of also being the punching bag (heavy bag) for my mother, if she had any problems at work or with any of her spouses I was the eldest, so I would absorb all that frustration.

I got beating for things I knew nothing about, I got so fed up and knew that getting out was my only option. I tried relentlessly to be on her good side, to get in her good books, to find some favor in her eyes so that it could help to alleviate the abuse, but I was never able to get there until I moved out and lived on my own. As an adult, I would tease her and say it is a good thing God was on my side or else she would have killed me… and this is just the plain truth because I attempted suicide on several occasions, but I guess I was not doing it right because I am still alive to share my story with you. There was one night that she walked into my bedroom and poured kerosene all over me saying she was going to catch me on fire.

One evening I was doing the dishes on the outside and a smaller pot got fastened inside her pressure cooker and in my attempt to remove the small pot out of the bigger pot (her prized pressure cooker) I had unfortunately expanded the width of the pressure cooker, so the cover of the pressure cooker could no longer fit the pot. I was so scared of her I did not tell her because I would have gotten a beating. However, she still found out and saw it fit that my punishment was to be burned in my sleep…at this time I was ready to die anyhow because I could not be bothered anymore.

This brings me to the point, that when you feel as if it is time for you to take your own life, then it is time for you to do a self-evaluation and look in the mirror and realize that the God of Daniel is bigger than any temporary problems that you have. It is often said that one has to be in your position to understand what you are experiencing, but if you should just decide to do a personal survey and get some persons to share their most challenging experience you may say two things; "that is a real hell to go through or Wow, I can't imagine how good I've had it"

I don't believe that not having a father figure created any impact on my life, in fact, I can't say if I had one it would make much of a difference. All I can say is that not having one for myself made me want to make sure my children have one of their own. Sometimes we pray and ask for things that we are not physically or emotionally prepared for. But does this mean we stop asking and seeking God's face? After moving to Kingston to live with my mother and other siblings it was one of the roughest times of my life but I believe that God was preparing me for something great.

People would think it was because of fear why my Mother behaved like that, and guess what, they were right. I think one of the reasons I was treated so badly was because I was the first child, I kept to myself because I did not want my mother to have another reason for beating the Jesus out of me, worst 'I was the reason her life was so hard' according to her. She had me when she was seventeen (17) so in her eyes, I made her life a living hell, which is so silly because with unprotected sex the chance of getting pregnant or disease is very high. So I could not understand how I caused her to make that decision, besides, she gave me away when I was three (3) months and I never asked her for anything. Even when I was going to school, I did not ask her for lunch money, if I did not see it on the table I would leave the house without it, so I believe that it was my mere existence that caused me to be on her bad side. When I look back on the physical struggles that I went through I knew I should have died, in fact, I am only alive at this moment because God kept me. I ran away from home because I was being abused, the home should be a safe refuge for anyone but for me, it was the most stressful environment.

Sometimes we may find ourselves just wanting to get away, to be removed from a situation, but let me inform you that this stage of our life is necessary. We encounter challenges so we can build our true character, "Beautiful souls are shaped by ugly experiences" According to Matshona Dhliwayo.

Have you ever seen the process to make wine out of grapes? These grapes have to be beaten or crushed, note that these grapes can either be picked by machine or by hand during the day or at night to maximize efficiency, 'beat the heat and capture grapes at stable sugar levels' some farmers would say. So, your challenges will not show up when you are expecting it. It will just pop up at once and you are expected to be ready to handle it. Now, these grapes are picked with their stems, with the expectation they will eventually be removed. These grapes are pressed to extract the juice and leave behind the grape skins. The pure juice is then transferred into tanks where sediments settle to the bottom of the tank. After a settling period, the juice is then "racked", which means it's filtered out of the settling tank into another tank to ensure all the sediment is gone before fermentation starts. And even going through all those processes, this juice or liquid is still not considered to be wine. So don't dwell on how challenging your life has been, sometimes you may have no choice but to go through the process to get your breakthrough.

A change is coming it will change you but how much are you willing to encounter to appreciate the change when it comes.

I would get beaten for things I had no control over, I used to believe that perhaps that's her way of giving me attention, God knows how much I hated that type of attention. Sometimes I would be so scared to go home, when I got in from school I would fall asleep at my gran Aunt house, instead of walking over to my place which was less than a minute away, as we were in the same tenement yard. I could only wish for the mother and daughter relationship that is often mentioned among my peers. Through all of that, presently I still manage to stay by her side despite the treatment I was given.

Imagine as a teenager how embarrassing it must have been to be constantly humiliated in the presence of your peers, living at Maxfield Avenue which is in the heart of Kingston and living in a tenement yard. To give you an idea of the setting, picture this, nothing is sacred in the surrounding, everyone knows what you are eating, what is happening in your bedroom and even when you used the bathroom to relieve yourself. As the community was small, everyone knew what was going on with you and your family. This was like having the internet at your fingertips, but during this time we had no such access, so word-of-mouth was the tool used for sharing information.

One day I got so frustrated and decided that I had enough, filled with tears and sadness I knew in my heart that I would not take the beating anymore. So that same evening, instead of running and hiding, I ran so fast away from the house that I am still not sure when I stopped running. Not knowing anywhere outside of school and home at the time, I ran that night until I was tired, when I eventually stopped running I ended up in Coronation Market in the City of Kingston which was approximately an hour away via transit. Only God knows what was lurking in the night streets but he kept me safe and from then I knew he had his angels over me up until now. I met a market vendor who made me sleep on her loads that night and the following morning she took me to the police station, Denham Town Police Station.

God has a way of showing up in your life and he always does it through the most unusual medium. He will manifest himself when you least expect it, if you should look at some of the most difficult times you have faced in your life and ask yourself, how did I do that? then you will understand that He was the reason you made it.

He will place even your enemies in situations to bless you or to take you out of danger. I have learned never to underestimate the power of faith and how protected we are when we believe. He will make a way when you can't see any way, it is not your job to ask how it is going to happen just believe that it will happen. I have proven him so many times, when I look back at that night when I ran away, as a young girl I should have died. I was barefooted and had only my yard clothes on, so I was unprepared for any challenge I would have encountered.

Sometimes in our lives, we get so discouraged and frustrated that we believe the only way out is to give up, run away or even kill ourselves. We haven't completed our process on earth as yet, we are not yet wine so hang in there, you are just around the corner to be a pleasure for someone's delight. Never allow anyone or anything to make you want to end your life, it's not worth giving your life to make anyone else happy.

If you want to give your life, give it in service for something great and make it meaningful. Do not give in because you felt that you can't take the pressures of life. Pressures are what will take us to a perfect state, for example, I always look at a pressure cooker and the impact that it has on the most difficult meat to cook. It would take a few minutes to cook to perfection but regardless of the amount of time that meat took, it will come out easy to bite. So do not give up under pressure but instead fight and push your way through. Your surrounding should never dictate your future directions, so use your words to succeed at being yourself. Never say or think negative things about yourself such as 'I never do anything right' or I will not make it'. My favorite book said, "by your words you are justified and by your words you are condemned." If we practice to speak good things about ourselves and declare positivity over our lives, we will be shocked at the outcome. In the Garrison or the Projects, I chose a different direction for my life, even though society told me what they believed I should be.

We lived in a Tenement Yard similar to how Bob Marley describes it but the difference was that my yard had two gates, each on a separate street and these streets were often at war with each other. It was both a blessing and a curse to live in that setting, whereas if one street was flaring up, we had the option to enter or exit through the other street. There were eight (8) families that occupied the property, each household consists of at least four (4) persons, we had two (2) toilets and two (2) shower rooms. These rooms were strategically placed at separate locations because of the number of persons that lived at the property. My mom shared a common area (hall) with three (3) other families, it was used for our kitchen, so we all had our stoves in that area, because of how the hall was designed we all had to wash the dishes on the outside. So, each family had their section outside that they used to do their dishes, meal preparation and laundry amongst other things.

As a result of the size of the hall, each family was only limited to having their stove and counter table for storage. We had drums and barrels filled with water because at that part of the city running water was inconsistent. When we do get running water from our pipes, we had to stay up for hours hoping that the 'water God' (National Water Commission -the public water system of the island) would bless us for a little while. For months we would go without getting water in our pipes so we had to fetch water from different communities using creative means. This became a chore, so as children we knew that the drums had to be filled daily, we needed water to flush toilets and to help with basic needs. One of our neighbors had a 'handcart' in the yard so we would pack the cart with several buckets and bottles, as long as it was considered as a container that can hold water we would pack it on the cart. The size of each family made our task even bigger, this was because we would have to make several trips to get one drum filled. We would spend approximately six (6) hours daily only to fetch water. If your children did not experience this, share this story with them because even now in Jamaica and in other parts of the world some families still have to fetch water and keep in storage for daily usage.

We did not know about the importance of washing hands after using the washroom, merely because we could not afford to use too much of the little water that we had. We knew we had to save and stretch the amount of water in each drum. Some of our neighbors would secure their drums by putting huge stones and even locks on them to ensure that others did not interfere with their property since this was a common thing to do. When we were doing the dishes, it was the norm for all of us to have two (2) containers one to wash and the other to rinse, when we were done with this water we would store it for use in the toilet. That was an experience that built me and I believe that it has helped me as an adult, I have learned to appreciate and be grateful for the things we often take for granted. Look how important it is to wash your hands, can you imagine? because we had a fear of wasting water we did not do this important act but this was second nature to us. As children sometimes we would get so sick and did not know what was causing our illness, but when I look back, I think that it was our immune system being built from all those possible diseases that we may have come across.

Funny enough, despite not having tap or clean water in the countryside, I never got sick until I lived in Kingston, and Kingston was said to be the better way of living. When I moved to Kingston I would catch it all the viruses or disease outbreaks that occurred; measles, chickenpox, mumps, you name it, I would have gotten it. They would tease me and call me 'the collector' and that name stuck on me for a while until one day one of the older ladies explain to me that is it because I came from the 'country breeze' and my system was not used to the 'Kingston breeze'. Of course, I believed her because, at that point that was the best explanation that anyone could have given me, even though we lived about a half-hour from the hospital I was never hospitalized, I guess the 'Kingston breeze' did its course and several years later I am fit as a horse. It is funny how a change will affect your condition, but when you condition yourself for a change the result you get will determine your divine destiny. You cannot always change your outcome but you sure can manipulate what you would want your outcome to be. Think about this, you find yourself struggling to pay your rent, but you need food for your children, you have a good relationship with your landlord and you are not normally late for payment but there is a strict policy that if you do not pay your rent on time you will be evicted, how would you manipulate your outcome?

Chapter Six

Hopeless yet Relentless

At the age of twelve (12) I was enrolled in the community all-age school, my grades did not meet the current school standards, so getting accepted posed a challenge but then again God showed up and handled His business. Mother was not a patient individual, she was one of those persons that love when things are smooth, in other words, she will get mad for no reason, but weird enough she showed more concern for me than getting angry at me for being so academically challenged. Even though my grades did not meet the school's standards God was in the midst of it, I got in through the recommendation from a friend of a friend of our neighbours. When God is ready to move in your life, He will move all obstacles out of your way, He will even create new avenues to ensure that his people are not left behind. He will call your enemies to bring you blessings, sometimes you will see doors opening, and you will find yourself moving into seasons that you could never fathom.

There is this belief that you have to have a certain level of education to be successful or get a certain job but I have seen where people are not qualified for certain positions and hold that position very well. Do not downgrade yourself because of your intellectual capabilities, God uses people of all types to do his mighty work. He will create positions for you where qualifications won't matter. Do not get discouraged if you find yourself struggling, just don't give up, push past your pain, it may seem hopeless but fight and align yourself with persons who can help you, never be afraid to ask questions, develop an 'I do not care what people think of me attitude' and push yourself.

After starting school, I managed to capture the attention of some teachers who believed that I had potential and they worked with me. If God has his hands on you then no Demons from hell can hurt you, I'm not saying that challenges won't come but they are only there to make you stronger. When you find yourself in unbearable situations always compare where you are coming from and where you are heading. God has a way of placing things and people in place for you, and all these placements are there for a specific reason that we may not understand. In my case throughout all-age school Miss Rohael Johnson, a teacher from Africa saw something in me and under no circumstances would she allow me to quit, she mentored me up until I completed all-age school and when I moved on to High school she was still available. She was my "go-to" for everything, she exposed me to potentials that I did not know existed in my life, she took me in her arms and refused to allow me to settle for anything but the best. She taught me how to have an "I do not care what you think of me" attitude and I have mastered that throughout the years, it has pushed me to so many successes.

I find that our biggest hindrance is ourselves, we allow persons to control our thoughts and beliefs which in turn deflates our potential.

She would have classes at her home on her veranda free of cost for some of her students. I was not always in her class but I would show up regardless. She would never turn me away and while she was teaching, her mom was preparing meals for us. Even when I was no longer in her class, she would still provide some level of academic assistance to me, if she was uncertain about a particular subject area, she would ask her sister or brother-in-law to help since the internet was not so popular in those days. I always enjoyed going there because her family was so close-knitted and they were brilliant so I thought I could learn a lot just from being in their company. It's just natural that if you want to be successful you have to surround yourself with successful people.

When I think about the goodness of God and all that he has done for me, looking back on my life I cannot truly count all the Angels that were place on earth for me.

While having the challenges of coping academically, I was not getting any help when I got home with school work either, so I had to try and figure out everything for myself. I was the eldest so my responsibility at home was to ensure that my other siblings were ok. This is by helping them with their homework, cooking, cleaning and washing until our mother got home. I spent more time taking care of them and the house than taking care of myself and because of that mindset when I got married, I found myself doing that as well. When my age group was playing or going to parties, I had to stay home and do what parents are supposed to do, so I believed that my childhood days were over at age of eleven (11).

I was scared of my mother so my first reaction was always ensuring that everything was taken care of before she got home. I remember a particular day at school we had a class party because it was the end of the school term and we got lots of candies or sweetie as we called it then. So, I took some home for my siblings and later that evening we started eating them and my mother asked us where we got them. I told her how I got them, but she did not even allow me to finish explaining to her, I immediately got hit in the face; I fell on the ground and she came on top of me and started hitting me all over my body. My mother weighed anywhere between two fifty to three hundred (250-300) pounds and I was just a little skinny kid…

In our world today, children are empowered to call the police when they are grounded or when they feel they have been mistreated; but back in those days when parents are reprimanding their children, it is as if they are at war, anything they can reach at arm's length became a tool of danger, to cause harm to the child, at least this was what I went through as a child. I currently have scars on my body to show how I was abused but through it all, I knew that scars do not reflect where one is heading. I now treat my scars as reminders of what I have been through and how I overcame them. From that day until now I lost my appetite for sweets, so I do not eat chocolates or any form of candies because in the back of my head I still believed that my mom is going to smack the Jesus out of me. Some would say where was God in all of this? But I say He was there, that's why I can share my story.

Every testimony comes from a test in life so to share you have to have something to share about. I hated my mom growing up; there were days and nights that I thought of several ways to take her out or get rid of her but that's not me, that's not what God has intended. It was obvious to everyone in the yard that she mistreated me, our neighbours would talk to her but instead of her behavior towards me improving, it got worst. The worst thing you can tell a parent is that he or she is not doing a good job at parenting. In this case that was my mother's story, the more criticisms she got, the harder my life became. I would get everything if she had a bad day at work or had problems with any of her boyfriends 'I would feel her wrath' according to her. I was so scared to screw up at anything that I never even had a boyfriend as a teenager; I knew she would kill me if she found out, so I stayed away from boys or anything that looked like them.

In the 90's the Ministry of Education had this program in schools called "Common Entrance", this was an examination that children would take to obtain placement in a high school. Of course, I was told that if I did not pass the examination I should prepare to move out. Where would a fourteen-year-old with no father move to? So nevertheless I was always verbal and I told my teacher, Ms. Johnson, at the time, she told me not to think about her (my mother) when I'm doing the exam, she also sarcastically said whether you pass or fail it will be a 'win-win' situation.

To me that was comforting because I knew that someone had my back; when you know that someone has your back it's one of the most comforting feelings anyone could ever ask for. I knew then just as I know now that God never gives us more than we can handle, He promises never to leave us neither forsake us. I believe that He is the same God yesterday and the same God today, we may not get what we want when we want it but He is always on time. Sometimes all we need to do is to exercise a little patience.

I questioned and cried several times and asked God why me? how did I end up in this life, I used to believe that I was adopted because no child should be treated so harshly by someone who carried them for nine months. I have learnt that it's a fact that when all hope is lost, God always seems to find a way of reminding us that we are never alone despite our situation. I used to believe that I was the only one who faced tough situations but I realized that everyone you meet is fighting a battle you know nothing about, so sometimes we make the mistake of putting our conclusion on things when God already put his conclusion on the situation. This can cause us to be frustrated and think nothing is working out for us but we just need to believe wholeheartedly and we will be surprised at the outcome.

It is so hard to learn how to love without condition, talk without bad intentions or even give without reason so what we do is fight to feel appreciated or do things to get recognized. Sometimes the things we do to impress persons happen to be the biggest mistake or even the greatest gift you have ever given yourself. In my case I was desperate to fit in and to be loved by the only parent I knew so I made a conscious decision to get baptized at the age of thirteen (13), I knew that my mother got baptized a few times and was backslidden so I felt that being a Christian at that age she would be happy for me and encourage the move. But was I up for a surprise? It was at this point in my life I realized that my mother's behavior is one of the many things she had no control over, everyone had a role in life and I believed then and now that her role was to make me the woman I am today and this was through every wicked and dreadful act that she put me through. She discouraged me from baptizing but, of course, I went ahead and did it because something inside of me was telling me, that this was the direction to go, I had zero regrets.

I was never a child who has a lot of friends or waste time playing on the street, it was school or church for me and then straight home. I used to believe that my mother was so paranoid because when we wanted to go to church in the evening she would not allow me to go unless I had adult supervision, even though the church was ten minutes away from where we lived. She may have had good intentions, but she only knew that way of how to raise me. I prayed relentlessly just to be able to have a conversation or even to get a smile from her, however, the first time she told me she loved me was in my mid-twenties. That is the relationship we had, those family trends or some would call it 'generational curse' were things I made my point of duty not to happen with my children.

It is every girl's dream to be able to sit down and talk to her mom about anything without being judged but in my case, that was a dream that was far from happening. While I was going through puberty, instead of learning about my body from my mom, I learnt about it through books and guidance counselling classes at school… thank God for that. When I started menstruating and was not sure of what to do, I called my mother and show her what was happening to me, instead of her explaining what was happening I ended up getting threats from her. Her exact words to me were 'I'm now a big woman so I can go and 'take men' now and she will know what to do with me" if your parents are Jamaican or you have any knowledge of "Jamaican parenting" you will understand they can be very sarcastic and they use a lot of scare tactics as a part of their parental development. So, I knew that statement was a direct threat to stay away from the opposite sex. I was uneducated and scared, I was convinced that looking at a boy would get me pregnant, and because of the fear that was implanted in my head, I would close my eyes at boys because of the fear that any direct contact with the opposite sex would get me pregnant. "Peppering my crotches' (throwing hot pepper sauce in my genitals) was a famous line that mother often used, not sure where she got that, but those were some of the words I grew up on. But throughout it all God has always had my back,

He never leaves me and many times when I felt like it was only me in this world, he always showed up for me.

We often believe that our past or our parents determine what we should become in life when in fact we have control over our lives. We sometimes believe that the government or the social environment influences our future or our dreams but I believe that we are what we are when we decide to be who we are. I often heard people make excuses and say we have to live a particular way because that's how we were brought up or that it is what we are used to, this is a lie from the pit of hell. The sooner we can understand what makes us happy and what makes us sad the sooner we will understand what and how we deserve to live our lives. No matter what you are attempting to achieve, it will not happen without sacrifice, hard work, a positive environment, a positive mental attitude, passion, determination, meditation, introspection, prayer and vision. Never use the word 'try', just do what you need to do to get to the next step. Do not make excuses, do not blame others, do not blame your circumstances.

Take personal responsibility, surround yourself with good people and let go of anything or anyone who tries to stop you from doing what you need to do to become the best you, and be aware of distractions because they are everywhere and these are some of our biggest giants.

Chapter Seven

The Breaking Point

When I left all age-school I was expecting big things to happen for me, sometimes in life what we expect is not always what we get but how we deal with it makes the difference. High school was a journey; I am however grateful that I managed to get in. Someone once said, "Expectation is the root of all heartache." The quote recognizes that when we experience disappointment, our hopes and expectations are out of line with reality. We all feel this way from time to time, some of these disappointments will not make much of a difference, but some disappointments can change the course of our lives.

Given the convoluted nature of desire, there are no experiences that are entirely free of disappointment so we need to keep this in mind. This is what makes disappointment such a complex and confusing feeling. Many of our desires that we pursue are unconscious, sublimated, and frequently contradictory if you have to think about this take a few minutes and do a quick self-evaluation.

Like many in my time, I would go days without lunch or even travel allowance to school, not only because my mother couldn't afford it, but that was just a part of my battle that I had to face. One thing I am certain about was that I knew I needed to get to a breaking point, so I was very active at school. I tried pretty much everything just so I could see what I was good at and also to keep me busy from all the drama that was happening at home. I felt that wherever I went I had to be remembered, yes, I felt that someone had to be touched even if it's just by my presence, this was instilled in me by my Grandmother and I ensured it remains that way. I would go days without lunch but still, I was never absent from school because I knew how valuable my education was. I knew what I wanted and I tried so hard to get it with or without a full stomach.

I had a passion to learn and a burning desire to excel because I was told and constantly reminded that by age seventeen (17) I would have gotten pregnant and dropped out of school and never become anything good in life, but my determination was never to end up like my mother. I wanted her to eat her words so badly, that I did courses that I had no idea how I would pay for them in examinations. I worked tirelessly to get good grades so that the teachers could recommend me for the final Caribbean Examination, which eventually came through.

Never underestimate the power that you have, whatever you believe in do not stop working at it until you get it. My situation made me start my day in the right frame of mind. I would tell myself that I need a change and I will not be depressed, so I practiced to be grateful. It is impossible to be depressed and grateful at the same time as these two emotions can't reside in the same space. So, I remove all depression and issues causing me to feel that way and kept focused and busy on what I knew was ahead.

I took all these courses in school, not knowing how they would be paid for, but I was convinced that something must happen. Keep in mind that 90% of the time I'm at school hungry. My strategy worked regardless; I got the go-ahead from the teachers to do the course so the next challenge was just to finance them. In those days, you can't participate in an examination without paying for them. God again showed up, in an unusual encounter, which up to this day, I am not sure how it happened. I was involved in the community youth program and I built up the giant urge to speak with the Member of Parliament for the area. I gave him all the examination registration information that I had received from school and told him that they have to be paid by a specific time and I have no one else to ask. He took the document from me and he said 'ok', I never saw him again and all I know was that I showed up for my examinations and was successful. People often talk about having crazy faith… I have lived through it. I have seen where I was at my breaking point on several occasions and God aligned things for me. Just when you are about to throw in the towel that's when you are about to get showers of rain, hang on to that towel a little bit longer.

God always answers prayers so trust him and be careful of what you asked for, he will give it to you whether you expect it or not. I was blessed with another teacher who was assigned to my grade from the first year up until I graduated; his name was Orland Claire, this man invested in his students. He never taught me, the only relationship we had was that he was responsible for marking the register and updating us of any changes in the school. He knew when I had no lunch for school, he knew when things were not going well at home and he knew all my teachers, it was then I truly acknowledge that there was a God and He will never leave his children hanging, this man was seeing through all my fakeness and my pride. Hungry would be killing me and I would never ask for food. I learn to survive on not having anything and then sometimes when no one is looking I would go in the cafeteria, pretend as if I'm helping to 'clean up' just so I could have something to eat.

When you feel as if it's time to give up please do not because just when you are about to that's when you may receive your breakthrough. There is a reason for every struggle in our lives and someone somewhere is assigned to help you to go through your struggles. Did you know that you are assigned thousands of angels to take care of you each day? Just imagine how powerful you are when you can just dispatch them how you see fit!

Let me tell you, getting discouraged is inevitable, it is natural to feel that way but it's vital for you to push harder when you have nothing left inside. I managed to get all my subjects paid for I still do not know how but I know that God showed up. He said he will grant us the desires of our heart and one of my desires was to be the first out of my family to have a tertiary level education, which I was able to accomplish. I needed a passing grade in Mathematics to get into university so I never stopped until I was successful in getting that, I failed the subject three (3) times before I got the accepted grade for University.

I worked and sent myself to evening school, implemented rigid saving plans for university and at the same time was taking care of my household needs. I looked back and wondered how I was able to live on such a small income; but then I compared myself to other persons and was able to see that they are surviving on less than I had and they are able to do more than what I was doing. The human part of us tends to look at what we have and complain instead of look at what we have and give thanks and see how we can make the best out of what we have. One of the things that pushed me so much is the story that is often told about the man that was about to commit suicide because he was so frustrated with life. He climbed into a tree with a rope around his neck getting ready to jump, but before he did, he decided to grab a quick snack. He ate a ripe banana and threw the skin on the ground; he looked down only to see a gentleman eating the skin of the banana that he had just thrown out. He then realized someone else had challenges far worse than he had.

Once you have made a provision to get to where you want to go then the only person who can stop you is you. I never started university immediately after I left high school why? Because of two reasons, I couldn't finance it and I was not academically qualified for enrollment. But that never stopped me, in fact being unqualified and poor pushed me, I knew I wanted a change from my current situation and choosing prostitution or 'finding a man' to help financially was not an option I was going to take.

If you know what you want, get up, and go hunt for what you want, too many times we rely on "hand-me-downs." I made myself qualified and it was hard and painful. I bawled, I got a lot of no's, I sought financial assistance through various companies and even politicians, I applied for a student loan and was turned down by the government, they told me that I was not qualified to receive assistance because my assets did not meet government standards. Why would it be, I was living in a 2-bedroom board house with my mother, she was earning below minimum wage and I had no father.

When you find yourself between a brick and a hard place look closer at what you have and use it. If you are not able to move or see, shout until the people on the outside of your trapped area can hear you.

I chose not to make my current situation dictate my future outcome negatively. You will be judged based on your social background, your complexion and even your sex. I was deprived of educational opportunities; my mother was constantly relocating residence. I was categorized as being from the "ghetto', no child should be judged based on their surroundings or the background of their parents and I was a victim of that. Nevertheless, I chose not to let it impact me negatively.

Some of my peers dated older men for various reasons, some ended up with three (3) children before they got to the age of twenty (20), some died, some got various Sexual Transmitted Diseases (STDs) and some went to prison. What does it mean when you find yourself saying—or thinking—"I can't take this anymore." We've all been there, yet these words do not mean the same thing to everyone. People reach their breaking point in different ways, according to their personalities. A person who balks under pressure may just stop responding entirely. Another person simmers, and then suddenly explodes. Everything depends on how you relate to stress because reaching the breaking point happens when your ability to cope with stress breaks down. When I am challenged that's when my inner beast comes out.

We've all used the word stress a lot, but most of us haven't looked at our stress response very deeply. Take these moments into consideration. Breaking point 1: You are aware that you are under pressure, but you still feel centered and in control. Breaking point 2: Stress has got you frazzled, so you have to make a conscious effort not to respond with anger, anxiety, impatience or blame. Breaking point 3: You can't cope any longer, and you have an outburst, which releases tension momentarily but leaves you with feelings of embarrassment and regret. I know this is easier said than done but try to learn what it feels like to be centered, value this state and train your brain to stay there.

Being hungry to make it affected me, this was because though I was working, my mother lived in a two-bedroom board house with three (3) other children. That never stopped me in fact it pushed. Moreover, I could not get anyone to stand as collateral for me so I chose to put God to the test again. I went straight ahead and applied for University not knowing where the tuition fees were coming from, I believed that if I got accepted, then He will make me start attending school somehow and He was not stupid to make me drop out. Sometimes we have to exercise our faith and prove God for ourselves.

According to Jack London, 'You can't wait for inspiration. You have to go after it with a club'. Several times we find ourselves waiting for others or some miracle to make a move, then what happens is that we waste our talents or worst, the world left us there, still waiting for us to get our breakthrough. When I look back on how I was able to complete high school, I knew I had some hidden potentials. With all the challenges that I was faced with, I was still able to complete high school with a diploma and later on went to University, despite how society had labelled me.

I am a true testimony that great stories come from a challenging start; it is not how you get into the race but how you decide to complete it. Many times, we are in situations where to the bare eyes there is absolutely no way of finishing the race; but my word to you is at least enter the race you never can tell who is in the crowd cheering for you.

Chapter Eight

The Decision

Modern culture is set up to reinforce a kind of restless existence, it glorifies action for its own sake so that resting feels like giving up. You've heard of people who claim to thrive on stress, who exist on thrills and need barely four (4) hours of sleep. The reality is far different from the image, however being able to stay centered, relaxed and present is the optimal state of balance for mind and body. Being too stimulated even by positive feelings is stressful and unhealthy. This may become overwhelming and if you are not careful this may cause some level of acute illness in the body.

Your brain is used to the lifestyle you follow and has adapted to it. So, if you push yourself out of balance, the brain's mechanism for returning to balance gets worn down over time. This mechanism is powerful, every cell in the body wants to be in balance. My parent had a challenge in sending me to school; in my head, I sincerely believed it was pressuring for her as a single mother. She always had financial issues; I remember she would send me to one of her boyfriends to collect money for school. This was so annoying and scary because I thought the man was creepy, so when she thought I went to collect money for school I would go straight to school empty-handed. I had lots of pride and I was a feisty child, if you give me, I will take it but I will never ask for it and until this day I am the same.

For years I was walking Forty-five (45) minutes to school back and forth, but guess what, I was ok with this because this was familiar to me. For lunch, if it was available I would eat something, if not I would do without. I do not know if my mother was aware and I chose not to say anything to her. I got so used to it that it became a part of me. I was forced to take care of myself at an early age and as a result of this, it shaped my personality to look out for persons even when they do not deserve it.

As long as you are in the race, whether you can win or not just have a clear goal in your mind to complete the race irrespective of the position you ended up taking in that given race. They say at times it is the fittest of the fit that makes it through but based on experience, I believe that it's not about how fit you are it's merely about the willpower that you have. People will see you and think that you are equipped to handle the 'race' so they will try to compete with you or even hate you. But if only they knew that you are questioning yourself in the back of your head and wondering how on earth you ended up in this race. Run your race and be mindful and remember it's your decision and only you can finish what you have started.

If you are in business the ability to make the right decisions on a timely basis is what defines you. It's not a skill that anyone is born with, but you can definitely learn and improve on your habits over time. That is why it is advised to seek the assistance of mentors that you trust and not be afraid to ask for assistance from people who you know will guide you in the right direction. If you want to be successful, you have to align yourself with successful persons.

It's not easy to recognize what your true potentials are, as humans it's when we are at our worst that we really realize what we are capable of doing and how talented we are. Who are what do we blame for this neglected talent that we have? Would we say society, or our parents or merely because you perhaps were not given the opportunity to face challenging situations and overcome them on your own?

When we look at how life is currently, some parents work hard to ensure that their children get an education, certain luxuries such as the latest cellular phone, clothing and the best food. While for some they may never get that chance, it's a privilege to wear clean clothes and have clean water to drink. I had to settle for hand-me-down clothes, this was normal for me and I survived it; that decision was made for me and because of that I made it my decision that when I have children this will be a choice. We all have to decide at some point in our life how we want to spend the rest of our life. This oftentimes will mean the changes we have to make, the company we keep and the move we have to make.

As a kid we all had a vision, we had big dreams to pursue in life, and those dreams may fade with reality. But deep down you will still think about how happy you were when you thought about what you wanted then. For those dreams to be fulfilled, we must spend time in training and cooperating with God in a process of personal development. This process includes time, determination and hard work. This is at times looking beyond the obvious and making some serious sacrifice. Why is it that some people have to work so hard for everything while some persons just get it handed to them?

We use automatic dishwashers to clean our dishes and laundry machines to dry and press our clothes. We just press a button and a machine goes to work. But nothing is automatic in God's kingdom and also if you want to excel in life it doesn't come automatically. You can't fulfill certain plans and purposes without developing the necessary skills. If we look at the book of Proverbs, we read about the Ant how they strategize their moves, the struggles and obstacles they often face but they are unstoppable. Ants make up for their small size with simple determination and big decisions, so we can learn giant-sized lessons from them. We must be just as self-motivated and self-disciplined that's the only way anyone can't stop you, it's by removing your colony.

As you develop that kind of self-motivation and discipline to live by, go for what you want with Christ as your guide. Keep pressing on, grow in determination and watch your dreams come true, I promise you it will not be easy but it will be worth it. What

I often tell myself is that there is a process involved in every situation, and nine out of ten times the process is never smooth. But on the other hand, nine out of ten times the finished goods are always perfected. Sometimes we get so discouraged that we forget our own existence; I remember trying to kill myself so many times. I couldn't understand why was it that my mother hated me so much and why was it that I had to work so hard to get what I wanted. It was not until I realize that for me to be able to help someone I had to be tested.

So, my prayers automatically changed, I thanked God for my struggles, my scars and my upbringing. I asked God to help me to be what he created me to be and to fulfill the dreams I had in my heart and now I can see some of my dreams manifesting and I am confident that the rest is about to happen. I still have my vision board, I am so extreme that I have a vision black book, I walk around with a book in my bag that I do daily jottings on what I need to accomplish.

I realize however that in order for this to happen I needed him to Help me to stay focused and put in the time, determination and hard work necessary to grow and live accordingly. Our fore-parents normally say live good with neighbors because you never can tell when you need them to help you. Neighbors do not necessarily mean the person who lives next to you but it can be anyone that you see either daily or a stranger. Sometimes just giving a simple smile or encouraging word may come back around to you when you need it most.

I hated my mother for how she treated me as a child and as a result of that, growing up as an adult, I ensured that she regretted treating me the way she did. I took care of her, I made sure that she was never in need of anything, I believe that the best way to give revenge is to show appreciation and kindness. I have lived to experience my mom and other family members amazed at how I treat her but I am a strong believer in respect and dignity. I respected her; I may not agree with how she dealt with things but I do not believe in disrespect. I remember not speaking with her for a while because of how angry I was. I felt that it was safe for me to stay away than to be in her presence. I called it loving her from a distance.

Sometimes as people we should step back and examine our situation and try not to deal with our emotions at the forefront. When we are dissatisfied and angry, we make horrible decisions. Sometimes these decisions we make cannot be corrected, so I would always suggest love or stay angry from a distance. Do not drink your tea when it's hot, if you ever experience a scorched tongue you will understand my sentiments.

How do I love or get angry from a distance? It's easy, learn to operate in slow motion yet be effective with it. Because of how unhappy I was and I knew my mother's pattern I knew she wanted me out of her place. It was just a matter of when and how. So as soon as I was finished with high school, I knew I would be at the age that she had me (17). So, I started working. I would save my money and buy my furniture. I had nowhere to keep them so I paid stores to keep them for me (layaway). I made sure that the bills in the house were taken care of and my other siblings as well, and even to this point I was still not in her good books. Work in slow motion! Do things to satisfy God and then you will be rewarded. It is tough but the reward is priceless.

Eventually, I moved out at age nineteen (19) and my sister was forced to go and live with her father that was because she was a different case. Family to me is important, I am the one who always fusses when things are not in place. I also hate the fact that the only time family got together was for funerals or weddings so I felt the need that despite all of this drama I will still do my part. I felt the need that I had a responsibility to take care of her regardless of how badly she treated me. If she needed financial support, I would assist as long as I was able to. She knew she had that over me so she would use my brothers to get to me, but I still believed I had a responsibility being the eldest of five (5). We are so full of hurt as people, it's hard to get out of this place at times, trust me, it takes some serious level of maturity to get to a place, where those pain and scars do not bug you anymore.

One of the biggest fights we put up as humans is to run away or attempt to fight a losing battle. Why do that? Evaluate, eliminate and brace. Sometimes you win the battle when you do the opposite of what people expect you to do. If they expect you to be mad, be happy and enjoy it to the fullest; they expect you to be mean, kill them with kindness! Do the opposite and watch how God makes a 360 degree turn for you.

This is how it is believing it or not, we just need to exercise the freedom of a Calm, Cool and Steady Life. This is not easy but I feel that we are all fighters. There is always a fire in us and sometimes it only appears when we are at the loneliest and most depressing time of our life. The sooner we realize that people are born to be free and it's a gift from God then the better it will make us feel. The question is, are you willing to go through whatever it takes to be free, or do you want to stay in the mess you're in for the rest of your life? If you want to be free, the key is to start doing what God wants you to do, one step at a time, and you'll eventually walk out of your mess.

Overcome evil and anger by praying for those who hurt and abuse you. Counter feelings of selfishness by doing something good for someone else. Whenever the enemy tries to stir up your emotions, calm down and do what God has called you to do! If you think about it, I'm sure we lose a lot of blessings we never even knew about simply because we fail to do for others what we would like to have done for us. We always want to be blessed by others, but do we take the initiative to unselfishly bless them first? If your marriage, family, or friendships aren't what you would like them to be, you could turn them around by adopting this one principle right now. Work in slow motion, do the opposite of what they expect you do after they have hurt you.

You may have been waiting for your spouse to do something for you. Maybe you have even been stubbornly refusing to help a friend because you want them to help you first. Living this way can be selfishly comfortable, but things will never change until you decide to actively change them. It's time to swallow your pride and save your relationships.

Instead of sitting around, focusing on yourself, waiting for blessings to come your way, it's time to actively make sacrifices and serve the people God has placed in your life. Be a servant and make others the focus. Instead of feeling rejected and ignored, you'll be amazed at how your relationships improve when you treat others the way you want to be treated.

Chapter Nine

Exercising Patience

I often hear older folks say there is a time and place for everything under the sun, that saying never resonated with me until I became an adult. I needed an instant change and I did not want to go through the process I needed my breakthrough immediately. I have learned that there is a season to plant, a season to water and a season to harvest, the planting and watering required hard work, but without that work and patience through the growing season, there would be no harvest.

The reality of life is that we rarely want to wait for the necessary progress to reach the result. This impatience is something that is often tempered by maturity and wisdom. On the other hand, there is often a complacency that comes with age that can stifle potential growth. As humans, especially young people, we seem to want things to happen too quickly. We think all change is progress, but sometimes, as we get older, many of us are satisfied with the status quo. We forget that there is no progress without change. There is an even spot there somewhere. We must realize both. There is no progress without change, but not all change is progress.

I decided to move to Canada, I knew I wanted to get there but I had no idea how I would be able to survive. I had no family there and I was ignorant of what it would be like living in a foreign country. That's another thing, you can research as much as you can before making a move but when your foot hits the ground, what you research is not always what you get. So many times, you will prepare yourself to expect a specific outcome, but when that outcome manifests, it is like your world is turning upside down. It is just life; we find ourselves in jobs that we did not study for or jobs that we are overqualified for. When I migrated to Canada, I knew life was about to get better for me. I was like, God you are too good to me, I got here and I do not even know how I got here. God showed up in my finances, he placed people in my life to bless me. I push and I made it in a country where I believed that I would be able to build my own family and take care of the ones I left back home. I was qualified for good jobs, coming from my previous country and I knew the sky was the limit for me, so I was eager to make some papers (money) and hold some big jobs… boy!, was I up for a surprise. Little did I know that when I got to this new country life was just about to start.

Life was starting over for me, despite all my degrees, diploma and experience, to survive I had to do jobs that never in a million years I thought I would do. I started working in a factory, it felt good because in the back of my head the money that I'm working is way more than what I was getting in my previous country; it's not what I was used to but I did what I had to do, and I wouldn't change anything about the experience. Among myself in the factory with safety shoes and other protective gear on were doctors, engineers and teachers. We all had to go through our growing season because ultimately our harvest would be greater.

Imagine fresh off the Islands, I had big dreams and wanted to be able to make some 'real money' straight out of University, the desire and determination were at a high peak, I could not wait to get my feet wet. I busted out of the gates, eager and hungry to grow professionally and financially, unfortunately, my plans did not quite work out how I expected. I figured that now I would be able to have a decent income to be able to meet my many demands.

Think about being in my position… you are encountering the shock of your life and on the other hand, you have family back home who heard that you are in 'foreign' who started calling and making requests daily. You do not even know how these people have your telephone number but all of a sudden, they need help to do all manner of things and not once would they ask if you were ok.

When we are patient, we will develop a greater appreciation of our success when it happens; think about it, once this is practiced and a level of enthusiasm is maintained it is inevitable how pursuing our goals will become selfless. It is patience that reminds us that our hard work will pay off, and let's not forget that worthwhile goals take time to achieve. As William Shakespeare wrote, "How poor they are that have not patience! What wound did ever heal, but by degrees?"

I was not able to work for a year, I had no documentation that would allow me to work and study at the same time; there was no income coming in and I believed that surviving alone would be impossible, but God always had a way of working things out. I believed that he would never give me more than I can bear and he would never make me die of hunger or freeze to death. I thought I was prepared to deal with the climate… I wore so many clothes that I could not even bend if something fell from me, I was prepared mentally but not physically. Life will hit you hard and you may think you are strong and bold enough to handle it, but you may crumble. I bawled several nights; the snow wouldn't go away and I had no one to tell when I was hungry. I would pay for my rent and then I couldn't find money to buy food. I had to go to school because I couldn't work and the only money I had was already paid into tuition, but despite these many challenges I was planted, and my harvest was coming up. We may give up when we see no way out, it's natural to feel this way, but trust me, it gets better if you just hang on until you burst through your soil.

Sometimes you have to be scared to make a move and, in my opinion, I believe that you achieve more when you are uncertain of what the outcome will be. So frantically I began searching websites and sending out resumes to places that I never knew existed. I also joined a gym just to be able to start networking, I made flyers and posted them on elevator doors and bus stop signs offering baby-sitting services and homework tutorials and I also made business cards branding myself as a hair technician.

I lived in an apartment that was used for daily gambling, and there would be various men coming in and out of the apartment, so I decided to use them for my market, so whenever they showed up for their games I would cook and then sell it to them. These are talents I had but was never shared or even thought about sharing until my back was against the wall. After been enrolled in school, I later decided that I was going to do some research to find out exactly what Canada's economy was looking for so I went beyond what I had qualifications in and decided to study in a new field. I studied in health for three (3) years and even though I was registered to work in the health industry my permit did not allow me to. So again, it was another setback for me, during all this time I was financing myself through college and fighting to live on no steady income. As an international student, I was not qualified for any financial aid so I relied on faith, I was planted to be successful and I had all intentions of growing to full capacity. Like a plant, all you need sometimes is just someone to give you a little water and sunlight so that your leaves can breathe freely. When you are destined to grow you will find yourself protruding through the most difficult places.

I eventually had a wakeup call, because it hit me that nothing in this country comes easy and you have to start all over; I had to be strong enough to condition my mind to do anything as long as it is not illegal. At this point, I was hungry and occasionally was cotching between a 24- hour gym and a gambling house. Nevertheless, I was very proud through it all, you would never know what was going on with me. I chose to live as if everything was normal, I would dress up and clean up as if I have everything under control when deep down I was empty. When the gambling apartment got so noisy and violent, my hiding place was at the gym. I am thankful that this gym was 24-hours as I would spend most of my time there, just studying or prepping for church.

You look at someone walking around each day and you do not know what they are going through, or what type of mental state they are in. I remember I was at that place in my life where all I wanted was an opportunity to spread my wings. I never gave up, I continued to push myself and I am always comparing my life to someone less fortunate, so that always encouraged me. Sometimes we rely on people to nurture us when deep down all it takes is for us to apply self-care.

I acted like I had everything to make me happy. When I spoke to persons, I would speak positivity in their lives and the windows of opportunity started opening up for me. Jobs kept appearing and these were jobs that I was overqualified for on paper but I did not care, I intended to be able to get some finances in, so I worked and I worked. I never cared what my job title was, I needed the Canadian experience and I was bound to get it. I learned that if you are self-centered and arrogant you will never make it in this country. You have to be willing to do what you have to do if you want to eat.

It was becoming overwhelming for me at one point because I started to question my decision, I recognized that this was mostly due to frustration, anguish and pain; I would work so hard sometimes that my legs would be so swollen they can't fit in my shoe. I would have bunions on my fingers and at one point my hair started falling out. Regardless of this, I kept the faith and I fought my way out.

Do not get discouraged when you are struggling to see the light and no one will help you to get a peak, have you ever seen a plant that is all dried up? But when you try to pull it from the ground it is cemented in the ground that your natural hands cannot pull it out? You would have to get a spade or some form of tool to chop it out and even trying to cut it from the ground, you would still see stems from the root scattered all over the ground forming a new section to sprout up.

Do not count yourself out even when your leaves are changing color and starting to fall; if you can see the sunshine you best believe that there is hope. I recall praying to be able to provide for my family from a different country and God had blessed me with the opportunity and I was motivated that comes what may I would not be ungrateful. We get so ungrateful sometimes, we forget how much we prayed for rain and once it started raining, we complain about the mud and the potholes that surfaced.

So, I grew to understand and live with my mud, I embraced it and I used my puddles to soothe me when I am inflamed by society. God never gives us more than we can bear, so if we can handle the pressures, he will make you an example. I wanted to move to a foreign country and now that I had moved to one, I had to be able to be fit enough to face the many challenges that come with it. Persons looking at your life would think that you have everything going for you, people will even hate you because of what they think you have. But only if they knew how many sleepless nights you have had, and the racism, sexism and all sort of challenges that you had to face to get what you wanted.

There were times I got so depressed and overwhelmed that isolating myself was ineffective. I was already alone in this new territory and I had no one I could call for help it was just me and God on this journey. I had no family or friends in this country so I was already in quarantine. I knew my change was coming, however, one night I went back to the gambling apartment where I stayed and it was as if the roof was caving in, doors were breaking down, I could hear furniture bumping against the wall accompanied by loud applauds and profanity. Curious, I opened the room door and all I remember seeing was bloody men all over running for cover. I was so scared I immediately locked myself in the room because all this was new to me. I was not expecting things like this to happen in a foreign country. This clearly was the norm because, when these men are playing their games arguments transpire and the temperature of the room can change from a positive degree to negative in minutes. It was like Kingston 13 had landed in

Toronto with me where gang members were fighting for territorial privilege. I knew that I needed a change of scenery, so church was my go-to, and since this was familiar territory, I was enthusiastic about finding a home for myself. I needed a place where I could go to transfer all these emotions, to lay all these burdens as I was not used to being in a room with so much testosterone so it was beyond uncomfortable.

I tried to stay connected with friends and some family members back home, this would help me change my mind from the negative energy. Even though I buried myself in school and in work something was still missing. I remember I would go to church and I was hurting and no one knew or no one could see or even if they saw it no one said anything. I am strong, I am tough and I can handle anything; I do not need anyone, those are words that were embedded in me so I kept those words close to my heart. Until God showed up one day and said yes you are strong, but I am going to send you a comforter, in fact, because you have been so obedient I will give you several comforters, so you will never be alone.

I started seeing people walking into my life, doors being open and it was as if my life made a U-turn. I was blessed to meet an amazing gentleman who is now my husband; I was blessed with an amazing couple from the church I was attending, who became my friends and now they adopted me as their daughter. Now this couple has become my Pastors. I had no family when I migrated to this country, now I am blessed with a support system that I would never imagine. Trust the process, God is spontaneous, you just have to brace yourself, because you never know when He is about to flex his muscles.

People often ask me how did I do it, my answer has always been, so many persons wanted the opportunity to be in my shoes and since they can't fit in my shoe I am going to wear it for them. I decided that comes what may I would not let my temporary situation affect where I wanted to go. When the feeling of depression crept up on me, I started to recall all the times the Lord had shown himself to me and how much favor he had shown me, I realized that I knew the Lord is always teaching me through every battle.

He is capable of using our weakness to make us perfect, so sometimes when you find yourself in uncomfortable places, do not question it just appreciate it.

We need to know how to trust him and until we change what we believe in our head and heart we will never get what we really want. I had situations where I had to put God to the test, I was on my face and I nothing left in me; I knew that I am more powerful than I thought because I believe that if He is my Father then as his offspring I am a warrior. I grew up with little, so for me not knowing where my next meal was coming from or how I was going to be able to move around without a dollar to my name was the norm for me. I knew how to survive and turn my hand to make fashion as my grandparents would say. Our biggest challenge is that we fail to overcome from our experience, if you do not confront situations you will never be able to overcome them. You got to hold the bull by the horn sometimes as they would say.

Learn how to Love yourself, challenge yourself and push past what you think you are capable of. It's tough to enjoy life when you do not like yourself. People who haven't learned to accept and get along with themselves tend to have more difficulty accepting and getting along with others. I spent years having a hard time getting along with people until I finally realized through the word of God how my difficulty with other people was actually "rooted" in my difficulties with myself. I got burned so many times by persons that I automatically wear a shield, this is normal as I do not know who enjoys being hurt by other people. Even though it was instilled in me to be a strong woman, society at times made me feel as if my address should dictate the level of respect I should get.

We look for human validation so much, that we forget the true validator, which is ourselves, we are more powerful than we can imagine.

The Bible says a good tree will bear good fruit, and a rotten tree will bear rotten fruit. Likewise, the "fruit" of our lives comes from the "root" within us. If you're rooted in shame, guilt, inferiority, rejection, lack of love and acceptance, etc., the fruit of your relationships will suffer. Do not allow persons to validate you, based on your past or current circumstance. Even though you may not have a handle on things now, keep in mind that you are your own boss, act it, say it, believe it and watch it come to pass.

I know it's easier said than done as when I decided to migrate to Canada, I was not financially or emotionally prepared for it. I was in a relationship that I needed an 'out' for, for various reasons. I am my 'own boss' in my head so I did the footwork on how to leave the country and what the requirements were. I had to come up with two million dollars at the time in my bank account, this would verify that I can live and pay my tuition for the duration of my study. God showed up, I had a friend who made it happen for me, I remember calling one of my university buddy who I was travelling to Canada with and let him know my dilemma and his words to me was 'Anto I got you.' Isn't it a great feeling to know that you can just call on someone and they 'got you'? Now this friend of mine throughout university our friendship was just casual, we never had an encounter where we had to ask each other for anything. But look how God works, he aligns persons in our lives just when we need it and when we least expect it. I trusted my friend but most of all I trusted God. God never lies he got me and I was patiently waiting.

The time had finally arrived when we needed to approach the Commission to get the study visa, we both went on the same day, still no money. I did not panic, I was prepared to accept the Lord's will so I stood still and waited. Within the coming weeks the lord lined up persons who would show his favor, persons who would help me with the funds I needed and friends who poured into me, this was when I knew that God had me again. The major financial help came from a friend that I least expected it from; He was just a friend that I helped out once and I was just having an innocent conversation with him about leaving the country and he started asking me when I'm leaving and what he will do to help me.

Sometimes we are so conceited that we are afraid to share our concerns, but from experience, I have learned that you have to be led to share. Do not go around telling people your business who cannot help you or who will only discourage you from achieving your goal. You have to pray and asked God to put the right people in your circle. So many times, our circle is packed with squares and rectangles, until you recognize that something is wrong then you will forever have issues forming the perfect circle.

So, throughout all the busyness, it took me a while to realize that the Lord answered my prayers. It was not until one day while I was at home, I was calculating how much funds I had and how much I needed, that's was when I realized that the sum that I had written down was received. Immediately, I started bawling, these were graceful tears. I was so excited; I knew that my prayers were answered and that the figure that I had asked the Lord for was granted. So, I got the money that I needed to apply for the student visa. The enemy tried to play with my mind, tried to tell me I would not get the visa but I refused to listen to that voice and instead activated my faith with a bundle of patience.

With all of this, I was still in fear, I had mentioned to my spouse at the time that I wanted a change I even suggested that we do it together and start afresh. He was zigging and I was zagging; he never asked me how the process was going and I never told him. When I got back my passport it was never kept at the house, because I was not certain what he would do if he found out about it. We were living in the same house and it was the day when I was leaving the island, he knew about my travel plans. Are you believing God for some miracle in your life today? Do not stop believing, stay in faith and activate your faith daily. Remember that his plans for us are for good and not for evil, to give us hope and a future. I needed to act the way I did, I believe that if someone wants to make a change they will, no one has to hold them at gunpoint to do so. I reached a point in my life where I needed to do something but after analyzing the situation, making a decision may not be the right thing to do but when the inner warrior in you said make a move, you just have to make that move or risk living with regret and fear.

I was in a marriage where I was cheated on several times without explanation… not to mention the various abuses that came with it. I found myself making excuses for him on so many occasions that it started changing me as an individual. He lied, he had financial disabilities and displayed obvious signs that he was not mature enough to deal with commitment. We may believe that once we are married then life will be perfect as the fairy tales are, but we must understand… that's when the work starts. I have heard of couples who have been together for forty (40) years without marriage and once marriage gets in the picture then volcanoes start to erupt. On the other hand, we have people, that are married for years and they made it work despite the many challenges. One may say how can a woman stay in a relationship with someone who has repeatedly disrespected her? At what point do you say enough is enough? How do you know that when you go back into another relationship you won't experience the same problem?

These are some questions that you can only answer when you are in the position and you decide to make that decision on your own. People often say follow your heart but sometimes your heart is so broken that it is also indecisive. When your heart is telling you all sorts of things, what part of your heart do you listen to? No woman or man deserves to be cheated on but inevitable this will happen. Do you forgive and move on from there or do you start all over again? A friend of mine once told me that success is the sweetest revenge, I used my personal goals to make the decisions for me. If I find myself contemplating my next move it was always easy for me to fall back and ask myself what is it that I want.

I got to a place in my life where I would question myself trying to find out if I was the reason my marriage took the wrong direction. I would blame myself because I thought that I was too busy and because of this, he felt he had to get attention elsewhere. After doing a quick autopsy on my relationship and the life we had, I quickly rebuke doubt and self-blame. As humans, we do things because we want to do it, we are quick to blame others for our mistakes when we know that we put ourselves in situations. How is it an accident to fall into a long-term sexual relationship with other parties when you are married? How is it that it's an accident to hit your spouse repeatedly? And worst, how can you accept that accidents frequently happen and you must tolerate it?

We have to know when we are the victims versus when we are the victors, do not feel sorry for yourself, bawl, kick and scream if you must but do not allow anything or anyone to make you feel powerless. We often take responsibility for issues we needed to leave alone; we shouldn't allow someone else's behavior to change the person that we are. I believe that God allows you to go through situations that will help you to assist others who were also wounded. I never knew how strong I was until I encountered some of my most challenging battles. A spoiler alert though, sometimes you may think that you are prepared for the war, you planned all types of strategies to use on the enemy but on the day of the battle you may just end up losing a limb.

Just remember that it's ok to lose a limb, if you are not dead you will overcome. You will live to fight another day. So, dust yourself off pick up where you left off and start over if it becomes necessary.

My weakest times helped me to realize my true capabilities; there was a point in time that I felt armless in a boxing gage with Mike Tyson and Evander Holyfield. When I found out about my husband's infidelity I was studying at university. I was pretty much scraping through most of my courses but when I was experiencing my issues, I was getting A's in all my courses, in fact, I got the highest average that year of University. The point that I'm trying to make is that I had transferred all my energy into something that mattered to me. I knew that it was my responsibility to pass my courses, I was the one paying for school; I had to decide on dwelling in my pain or putting my shoulders to the wheel to get things done. Part of my heart was telling me to do things that would get me in prison and the other part was telling me to focus on me. Only you can determine your next move, you determine how you want to spend your life. We oftentimes live in another person's shadow, we are so busy faking it that we forget how to make it. I was so busy trying to make my former husband happy, that I forgot what makes me happy, so when all those situations came down on me it affected me so badly that I did not know how to handle it.

Patience is a virtue, it's hard to bounce back from a life that you have invested time, finances and emotions in. It's even harder if you knew you have given it your all only to find that someone ambushed you. After talking to several persons and experiencing it for myself it does take a sense of spiritual intervention to come back from a hurt such as this; it's like you were planted and just hoping for an outpour of showers.

Have you ever passed by some random dilapidated structures for years and you wonder how is it that this frame of a building stood still despite the harsh weather conditions? Think about it, these structures will not budge without some serious machine power along with manpower. This is because of the initial foundation of the structure. As individuals it's important that we evaluate our foundation, we must pay attention to our foundation so that we can stand up to the various conditions.

Chapter Ten

Nothing Just Happens

Never ignore someone beyond their limits, else they will slowly learn to live without you; notice when paper turns to ashes you are not able to burn it anymore. Sometimes you just have to accept the fact that things will never go back to the way they used to be and count either your losses or your blessings. Things happen but nothing just happens for no reason. We are destined to learn from our situations, this may be a good lesson or a bad lesson. I wholeheartedly believe that no matter what cards I'm dealt with; I am going to be successful. That's just how my faith is set up, that's how I was built. How were you built? Some of us are still trying to figure out how we were built and that's ok, but what about you deciding to plant yourself in a way that will make you happy?

It is said that successful people do what they need to do even when they do not feel like it. I have seen single mothers and fathers push themselves so hard to provide for their children because they want their children to have a better life than they did. So, toughen up, stay grounded and wait for your change.

I decided to move to Canada not knowing where I will go or who I will go to, but in my heart, that's what I wanted to do. I dreamt about it, I saw myself in the country but never knew how I would reach there. I truly believe that whatever you think about you will achieve. When I reflect on my life, I realize that I am blessed and God has been good to me; the ability to be able to provide for myself and family is a blessing, and this should not be taken for granted.

I have learned to believe that nothing happens by chance, so many times we are in unbearable situations but believe me that if there is a will there is a way. I got to a point in my life where I had to put me first, it's not selfish but in order for you to take care of the people around you must be able to take care of you. Do not confuse your path with your destination, just because it's stormy now doesn't mean that you aren't headed for better days. Just remember that outside energy has a lot to do with your personal goals, sometimes you telling people what your plans are will deter what your intentions are.

Be selective and remember that whenever God is going to elevate you, demons will come to distract you so you have to be focused and not allow these distractions to take you off your course. Each individual we meet daily is in our life for a reason or a season; I spoiled my ex-husband, I used to believe that men are easy to please. I had an open communication relationship where I would literally ask him; what do you want, is there anything else I can do? But then it hit me that no matter what you do for some of them, if they are going to go out and cheat nothing will stop them, this goes both ways. As humans we are not easy to satisfy, we become ungrateful and jealous, which is a demon and must be ridden of.

What do you do when you have done all you can and everything still goes sideways? The answer to that is do more, I know this sounds ridiculous but how else are you going to get the results that you want? Forgive and stand up for what you believe in! When I found out my husband had his many affairs, I used to look in the mirror and question how I looked, all my insecurities from childhood days started resounding in my head. I used to ask myself what was it that I wasn't doing, or could I have done something better? I questioned my physical appearance and even tested my mental capacity but then that tiger in me immediately stopped me and helped me to realize that all the things I did or that I was going through, He was preparing me for greater things ahead. It is ok to have that moment when your self-esteem becomes a point of question, but once you tell yourself that no matter how hard it is or how hard things get you will get through this.

Growing up as a young girl, most of us want the wedding and the white picket fence with a bundle of kids running around. To me that was the ideal companionship, I found my companion, someone who I would be able to start my life with, but little did I know that the challenges were just starting.

I got to a point in my life where I had to put me first. Taking care of others before me now became second nature to me, nothing or none else mattered but me. Life forced me to take up that mantle, have you ever been pushed so hard that you lost your balanced? Well, I lost my balance and I fell so hard on my buttocks that I was certain that I had experienced quadriplegic paralysis.

It's not easy to bounce back from hurt especially if you were ambushed by it; I have seen persons fall so far into depression and other mental illnesses; some people even became suicidal. It takes strength and God's grace to overcome pain and the unforeseen battles we face. Until we realize that as humans we are never satisfied, it takes some serious self-discipline; imagine yourself being in a buffet line with all your favorite food and you have a strict diet restriction due to medical reasons, how do you overcome this challenge? For me I had to learn how to prioritize, I had to decide to choose me and my happiness. Please note that this may be the hardest decision that you may have to make but in the long run it may very much be the decision that will end up saving your life. The stone that broke the camel's back for me was when he became physically abusive. It started with just simple restrictions such as handcuffs when he is being given the silent treatment. But then it escalated to me retaliating and went as far as pulling his firearm on him. I made a decision then that he will never put his hand on me again, I decided to choose life over temporary pleasure. It's never easy to walk away from something that you believe is good but sometimes these delicious delights that you can't have enough of are the same ones that may cost you your life.

In one of our marriage counselling sessions, I asked him why he cheated so many times and put my life at risk? Several years later he is still unable to answer. We always knew that we had issues such as finances and him not being a firm man of God as to how I wanted him to be. I was fooled in the beginning because he was a "Preachers Kid" and I was like, yes I won the spiritual lottery; I trusted God and I prayed like how a wife should pray and believed that a change of some nature would happen, but it never did.

I used to make excuses for him, saying that most men do not like talking about their finances, little did I know that you can't talk about finances if there is nothing to talk about. Yes, he had a very good job I believe, but I was not seeing the fruits of his labor. It is important that Couples talk about finances and sex before committing to marriage because these are red flags that will eventually lead to forfeiting.

We all have a role to play on earth and at times we have to decide what that role is; we get involved with someone who is not a team player and then we complain why it is that we can't win a simple match. Some would say how would you know upfront that they are not a team player? It's hard sometimes because people will fake as long as they want until they get what they want, it's like interviewing for a job you always wanted. You will say all the things that you think the interviewer needs to hear, you may even add the experiences and qualifications on your resume but when you get the job suddenly all the things you said you would do now becomes an issue for you.

So, the onus is on you as an individual to decide what you want, how you want it and with whom you want it. We live in other people's shadow because we want to be able to please someone else and in return, we end up being unhappy in the long term. Grace equals ability, God gives us grace to match our call and when we do our own thing, we do it on our own. When we follow His leading, He always supplies the grace and the energy to do what He's calling us to do. The best part is that while we do have to choose to receive His grace, we do not have to do anything to earn it. When you choose to follow God's call, He's ready and willing to help you. Jesus died to cover our sins so that we can walk righteously before God with access to the Holy Spirit who can help us navigate everyday life. Make sure you are in a position to receive His grace and ability, if you are trying to pursue your own path, tell God that you want to follow Him and ask Him for help. He will always be faithful to provide His grace to you (Romans 5:15).

I have nothing to gain by living a selfish life, instead of waiting for people to be good to me, I decided to be good to them first; treating them the way I want to be treated was one of my biggest lessons learned as a child. I mastered the art of learning from others mistakes and not rejoicing over peoples failure; nothing just happens, have you ever wondered how it is that trees can survive in rocky hills or how it is that the ocean can meet the lake and yet the quality of the water will remain the same?

If your marriage, family, or friendships aren't what you would like them to be, you could literally turn them around, it not easy but try to adopt these beliefs and principles. You may have been waiting for your spouse to do something for you, maybe you have even been stubbornly refusing to help a friend because you want them to help you first.

Living this way can be selfishly comfortable, but things will never change until you decide to actively change them. It's time to swallow your pride and make a move. Instead of sitting around, focusing on yourself, waiting for blessings to come your way, it's time to actively make sacrifices and serve the people God has placed in your life. I know it's hard to be a servant at times, but I have learned that once you start serving and not expect anything in return the universe has a way of making doors open that you were not expecting.

In Genesis 50:20, Joseph is speaking to his brothers, who had severely mistreated him. When they threw him into a pit and sold him into slavery, they thought they were working against him, but really, God had a plan to use those trials to promote Joseph to a place of great influence. Just like you who are facing various trials, God will use you. 'Nothing just happens' it is necessary for you to struggle. Sometimes the very things we think are awful, turn out to be some great blessings. The greatest trial can develop in you, the greatest faith, you might be at the bottom of a pit but

God has a plan to use that pit to promote you in His call on your life. Remember, God can see all, and He will use those trials for your good.

I almost gave up on several occasions, I made several attempts on my life due to the various stressors, but I overcame them. In the Islands, we would get heavy rains, and sometimes this would cause flooding and damages to property and livelihood. But what makes this experience so great is that the sun would shine radiantly after it all. I want you to keep in mind that your rainy days will not last forever, your summer is around the corner. So, fight against the spirits of suicide, fear, doubt and anxiety because you are powerful than what you imagine and you were born to manifest greatness.

When I was writing this book, I had to do a few interviews so I will share this story with you on how God will open doors for you that no one can shut. One day, Mr. Peter had a job interview to attend at 10 am but his wife developed birthing complications at 9 am. He decided to take his wife to the hospital and leave for the interview thereafter but on their way to the hospital, the taxi broke down. It was already 10:30 am before he could get another taxi. He arrived at the hospital at 11 am, checked in his wife and used the same taxi to go for the interview, he got to the interview location at 12noon, which was two hours later and he rang the bell but no one opened the door so he waited.

Earlier, however, the same day at 10 am, the company mail delivery rang the bell but no one opened the door either. When the door was finally opened, Mr. Peter said "I'm sorry, I came... " he wanted to apologize for being late, but the Secretary interrupted before he could finish his statement and ushered him to the Board Room. The Secretary said, "I apologize, Mr. Peter, for keeping you waiting since 10 am. We actually heard when the bell rang at 10 am but we were held up in a meeting with our company suppliers. However, we have sat since 8 am to deliberate on your job specification, your office and the salary." Mr. Peter was baffled and said, "Ma'am, I haven't been interviewed yet". The MD answered him and said, "We decided not to conduct the interview at least to save time and also save the interviewees money on transportation. So, we looked at the papers for the most appropriate person we wanted and we opted for you. Also, we had tested your patience this morning by keeping you waiting intentionally for two hours. That's part of your interview. You won't be disappointed, you'll be shown your office, your secretary and the driver assigned to drive your company's allotted vehicle and you'll be on probation for two years. On his way out, his phone rang and it was his wife, she said, "honey, I had delivered a bouncing baby boy." It was their fifth child and the only male child. He immediately named the child 'Miracle'. He got a double miracle the same day! All the disappointments turned out in his favor. God positioned the mail delivery man to ring the bell at 10 am, and God also held them up in the meeting until Mr. Peter arrived.

It's easy to doubt the process of getting your miracle, but I want to encourage you that when you have 'God kind of faith' nothing just happens. You will be surprised at how you will blossom into something amazing. I was held up by issues in my life and I was hoping that it might diminish; I thought that all my chances were gone, but He was playing favorites with me. God is waiting for you to release His favor, so do not go back along the way. Do not quit! Do not be upset by what you face along the way. God has already deliberated on your specifications. When you are qualified by God, you do not have to worry about any screening or interview process, He will put you right where He needs you to be.

It's true that we all still have a long way to go. I migrated to Canada on my own; I am the first in my entire generation to attend college and complete a tertiary level education, I trusted the process and believed that He will do what he says He would. I used to get discouraged about how far I had to go, and it seemed like I was reminded of it every day, sometimes every hour. I carried a constant sense of failure, a feeling that I just wasn't who I needed to be, I wasn't doing enough and I needed to try harder. Yet, when I did try harder, I only failed again and again.

I have lived from paycheck to paycheck, I have worked various jobs, I have cleaned toilets and wore heels and safety shoes; I have been fired, I have been abused physically, emotionally and financially but I will never stop fighting. Every successful story comes from pain and most times unwanted attention. Do not feel sorry for yourself because of your many failures, have you ever wondered why it is that an eagle will fly above the clouds when it rains while other birds will seek shelter? The eagle knows it's will power; he makes several attempts to get above those stormy clouds but he eventually does it.

It's only fair to now adopt a new attitude, "I'm not where I need to be, but thank God I'm not where I use to be. I'm OK, and I'm on my way!" I now know with all my heart that God isn't angry with me just because I haven't arrived yet. He's pleased that I'm pressing on and staying on the path. If you and I will just "keep on keeping on," God will be pleased with our progress. He has promised to light the path before us. We may not know the way, and we may stumble from time to time, but God is faithful. He sees your progress, He's proud of you, and He's going to help you stay on the right path. Do not get me wrong discouragement will come, but you must recognize where you are and where you are coming from and be grateful.

You have worked for years and gave it your best; you were never late despite the weather conditions, you showed up and one day you heard that your service is no longer needed or the company is relocating. The first thing you may attempt to do is worry or cry because you are uncertain of how you will provide for your family. Let me remind you of the children of Israel, the red sea in front of you and the army behind you. Trust God, he knows what He is doing; I am stubborn and I am my biggest critique and throughout the years, God had to lean me up against a wall and force me to remember that I am His child and he will never neglect me.

I had to pray several times and asked God to 'ambush me' because I know I am a seed and I need nourishing; I needed to feel and have sufficient evidence that He was around, I needed to see the purpose of my existence. I cried daily behind closed doors because I was longing for things to go my way. So out of frustration, I screamed for help and an ambush from the only God I knew. It was then, I saw doors opening, miracles creeping up on me, and the best thing about all of this is that when He ambushes you, anyone that you are in contact with will also feel the glory. When God gives you something NO man can take it away, do not allow anyone to make you lose your integrity even if you do not know where your next meal is coming from.

Never doubt what is in store for you, treat every encounter as a learning experience. I worked with a company and every time that we were supposed to get paid, we had to remind 'payroll'; it was so interesting that if we asked we would either get written notice from the employer stating that they are low on production, which would require them sending us home until further notice without pay or we would have severe disciplinary action brought against us. I thought this was the culture of working in a foreign country, disciplinary actions will consist of cleaning toilets or working in the freezer even though you were hired to work on a production line. Imagine, how do you work for months without getting paid? when you have bills to pay and children to take care of? I used to believe that this was my lesson on tenacity and endurance but again, God showed up.

The company closed down because the government found suspicious actions from the owners; all employees full-time and temporary were paid off and in advance and immediately another opportunity arose. This just proves that you find yourself in a situation that you may not understand but God is working overtime on your behalf, stop fighting your own battle, you are not qualified for that, trust me. People will come into your life for various reasons, some to teach you, and some to build you, so all you have to do is to make sure you position yourself to receive or refuse what is coming towards you.

People often say the 'enemy only comes to kill, steal and destroy' but until you have experienced it you will never understand what that statement really means. Now it is up to us to determine if we were going to let that happen, or better yet take what truly belongs to you. Irrespective of your beliefs, you will experience obstacles, so it is up to you to make a conscious decision on how to deal with it. Stop moving parts around, trust the process and allow things to fall into their rightful place.

Conclusion

This journey called life has its challenges, as an individual, you have to choose how to ride through it. As a parent, when you look at a newborn, you can just hope that he or she will be the best of everything, you want to protect them and create an environment that you never had. You want to put things in place for them, in the event that anything should happen to you, that they will be taken care of ……all this is necessary. But that newborn will start teething, their stomach will gripe, they will fall and may have some bruises or cuts, why? Because that's just life. However, as the parent, your function is to nurture and protect, you may try to prevent them from making mistakes or causing accidents but this may become a challenge at some point.

As you examine yourself, be mindful that you are a seed, you are powerful, you are destined for growth; you will become productive, you may not bear sweet or tasty fruit for everyone's pallet but you will bear. Make your way to the soil, if you are in a rocky place that's ok because some of the strongest trees are from a rocky place. Have you ever seen a spindly juniper tree? Most times these trees appear out of a crack or in a rock and all you can think about is how it survived being so thin with little or no moisture. Be willing to let go of what society tells you that you have to hold on to, be an eagle and soar until you maximize your capabilities. You may not have a crowd or any support system but trust the process and stand your ground and get planted.

Acknowledgments

This book was made possible because of the love and support of my family, friends and various earth angels. God has indeed been blessing me through all those who have made a positive contribution in some way, whether through encouragements or prayers. Thank you all, I am most grateful.

A heartfelt thanks to my husband who continues to support my vision in the best way he can. My business partners, my best friends and to the publishing team, you all have worked behind the scenes tirelessly to make this vision a success and I couldn't have done it without you.

Finally, a sincere thanks to my adopted parents/family, my treasured earth angels. I can always count on you to be my support. The day when I told you about my writing project you were as excited as little kids on Christmas morning and you were the proudest that I have ever seen you. You make my heart rejoice with thanksgiving constantly and your love has been a beacon in my life. My greatest appreciation to you for always having my back.

Made in the USA
Columbia, SC
09 February 2021